The Complete Book of
Dutch-ified
English

The Complete Book of
Dutch-ified
English

An "Inwaluable" Introduction to an "Enchoyable"
Accent of the "Inklish Lankwitch"

Gary Gates
Cartoons by Jeanine Wine

Good Books
New York, New York

Dedication

"This doesn't make any sense," an erudite friend told me when he read the title of this book. "Dutchified English isn't derived from the Dutch language, it's derived from the German language."

He's right, on the surface. The word Dutchified comes from the German word for German: Deutsch. Deutschified English becomes Dutchified English.

This book is dedicated to all those people who at first seem to be talking a little ferhoodled, but who on closer inspection make quite a bit of sense.

Good Books books may be purchased in bulk at special discounts for sales promotion, corporate gifts, fund-raising, or educational purposes. Special editions can also be created to specifications. For details, contact the Special Sales Department, Good Books, 307 West 36th Street, 11th Floor, New York, NY 10018 or info@skyhorsepublishing.com.

Good Books is an imprint of Skyhorse Publishing, Inc.®, a Delaware corporation.

Visit our website at www.goodbooks.com.

10 9 8 7 6 5 4 3 2 1

Library of Congress Cataloging-in-Publication Data is available on file.

Cover design by Georgia Morrissey
Cover illustration by Jeanine Wine

Print ISBN: 978-1-68099-037-9
Ebook ISBN: 978-1-68099-111-6

Printed in the United States of America

Taple uff Cuntents

Preface

Even presidents have funny accents.

When John F. Kennedy spoke Boston Brahmin, and when Jimmy Carter spoke Southern, they weren't laughed at. They were men who were true to their regional heritage. Their speech added to the richness of our American tongue.

However, if I would become president, I would be somewhat afraid.

I am a Pennsylvania Dutchman. I speak a variety of English known as Dutchified English, a mode of expression typical of my native region and German-Dutch descendants throughout the United States and Canada. Although there is considerable variation in the subtleties of pronunciation and syntax, there are three main components to Dutchified English: 1) English words that are pronounced with a German accent, such as "clod" for cloud and "crotch" for garage; 2) Words derived directly from the German that are unique to English, such as *rutch*, meaning to squirm, and *spritz*, meaning to sprinkle with water; 3) A German syntax that allows for usage of English words in creative ways, such as "the food is all" and "outen the light."

All my life my fellow Dutchmen* and I have been put down for speaking this way. In high school, teachers who came from other parts of the country would criticize the way we spoke. The pressure to conform to conventional speech patterns continued in college and after college by people who believed they spoke in a superior manner. Too many people have tried to make us feel like dumb, uneducated bumpkins. Too many people have tried to make us feel ashamed. Constant pressure is exerted on us to speak like most people speak—in a flattened-out, colorless, homogenized English.

Linguistically speaking, we are treated like second-class citizens.

Enough of this abuse!

Dutchmen, arise! Be proud of our distinctive speech! Our Dutchified English is a delightful, powerful, humorous version of English. Dutch power!

And to all of you non-Dutchmen, open these

pages and enjoy a good laugh with us Dutchmen. Our Dutchified accent is an accent on humor. And we love to share good things. We hope that in reading this book you will not only gain an appreciation of the way we talk, but also learn to enjoy your own version of English, whatever it is.

As you read this book you will not only learn how to speak better, but when an American Dutchman becomes president, you will understand him when he addresses the nation in Dutchified English.

May you laugh along with all of us Dutchmen in our Renaissance.

Being traditionalists, the speakers of Dutchified English understand "man" and its derivatives to be a "cheneric" term for "humankind."

How to Speak
DUTCH-ified
ENGLISH

Volume 1 (Vun)

Dictionary of Terms

In the Dictionary section of this book are sentences using only one, or a few, Dutchified words, so that the featured word is evident, and the contextual meaning clear.

Inevitably, varieties result. This is as it should be since diversity abounds in Dutchified English. The many regional enclaves of German-Dutch settlers throughout the United States and Canada, often heavily populated by the Amish and Mennonites, have their own varieties of Dutchified English. The localities, cities and towns within each region have their own sub-varieties. In Pennsylvania, people in Lancaster speak a form of Dutchified English different than that found in Lebanon or Reading. However, there is a common thread to all of them.

The more people distance themselves from their German-Dutch heritage, the less pronounced is their Dutchified English. But in distancing themselves from their roots, they create their own unique, individualized version of Dutchified English. An influence always remains!

A

A-1: A home sales company. "Ding Dong! A-1 calling!"

Abawt: Near, approximately. "That's abawt right."

Achey Belly: An upset stomach. "Lettie eats yogurt for an achey belly."

Ach: An expression of surprise. "Ach, that can't be so!"

Ackryculchur: The science of growing domesticated food plants. "The Amish practice a natural ackryculchur that will never wear the soil out."

Affritch: Common, typical. "He's just your affritch guy."

Aftawertz: Later. "We went fishing. Aftawertz, we had a fish fry."

Ain't: The proper contraction for "am not"; also used for "isn't" when it makes the sentence more powerful. "Ain't I smart? At least it ain't as bad as saying, 'Are not I smart?' "

Also means the end of. "To get to Samuel's barn go straight along this crooked road until the fence ain't and then turn left."

All: Finished; gone. "Is the turkey all?"

Also: "When the little red box comes then the train's all."

Altchebra: A branch of mathematics. "Pop! Guess what? I calculated the walue of Y in altchebra class today!"

Alumium: A metal. "We wrap our leftovers in alumium foil."

Alveese: All the time. "Vee alveese go to church on Sunday."

Amonk: To be with a group. "Are you amonk those who are coming with?"

Analysis: The author's wife's name in the present active tense. "My Mom's cooking the turkey analysis bringing the filling for Thanksgiving dinner."

Ankle: An approach; a vector. "A right ankle has ninety degrees."

Anudder: Not this one. "If your car breaks dawn, you can always get anudder."

Ape: A man's name. "Ape Lincoln saved the Union."

Apple Busser: A delicious brown spread made from cooked apples. "Spread me all over with apple busser a piece of bread."

Arawnd: On all sides of; abawt. "These youngsters sure get arawnd these days."

Are: Sixty minutes. "It'll take me an are to get there."

As: Instead of. "Nellie as soon would marry Paul as keep house for him."

A circle can be dewided by four right ankles.

Awch: A cry of pain. "Awch! That hurtss!"

Awt: The opposite of in; also to go unconscious. "He went awt like a light."

Ax: To pose a question. "I don't know. Why don't you ax him?"

B

Back: A paper sack used for carrying things. "My son likes to go Trick or Treating on Halloween and get his back filled with goodies."

Also a place where there's always more of something. "Eat all you like; there's more back!"

Bacon: The act of making bread and cakes. "Ann is a whiz at bacon cakes."

Bass: To clean or wash a person. "Be sure to give your daughter a bass before you put on her new dress."

Bat: Not good. "He was a bat boy yesterday, so I had to spank him goot."

Batch: A symbolic pin worn as a sign of membership. "When the cop showed me his batch, I answered his questions."

Beardy Men: Men with beards. "Married Amishmen

and the guitarists in ZZ Top are examples of beardy men."

Beance: A kind of food. "Beance sometimes eat out loud."

Bet: What you sleep on. "Paul was tired, so he went to bet early."

Bice: To purchase. "Emma bice her groceries at the farmer's market."

Binko Hall: A place where every now and then people yell, "Binko!"

Bissy: Active. "Are you bissy tonight?"

Black Bumper Gang: What some wags used to call some Mennonites because they painted their chrome fenders black. Now, of course, every car has black bumpers. Just goes to show the influence of a powerful idea.

Bleed: To argue for. "My lawyer is going to bleed my case in court Friday."

Bloss: A woman's shirt. "Her bloss is too bright for my taste."

Bond: Liable to. "With all his energy, he's bond to succeed."

Bop: A man's name. "Do you like Bop Jones?"

Bookie: What you sometimes find up your nose. "Jacob threw a bookie on the floor! I saw him too!"

Bose: Inclusive of two things. "Used to be I couldn't say norse or souse, but now I can say bose."

Cherry britches the cheneration gap.

The Complete Book of Dutch-ified English

Bra: The forehead. "A farmer earns his money by the sweat of his bra."

Braince: Head noodles. "Use your braince; don't waste them."

Brawn: A color. "Sally always wears a brawn dress to bake pies in."

Bray: To talk with God. "Most people only bray to God when they're in trouble."

Brink: To convey; to carry. "We're brinking the cheese. What are you going to brink?"

Britches: Structures people use to cross rivers. "Lots of old britches are decaying and aren't safe to use anymore."

Brunts: An alloy of metal. "In history class ve learned about the Brunts Age."

Bruise: A man's name. "Nellie buys all of Bruise Springsteen's alpums."

Brutz: To pout. "After our son was spanked, he brutzed for ares."

Buck: An insect. "I hate it in the summer when all those bucks smash against your car. It's tough to wash them off."

Bull: The opposite of push. "I can bull my own weight arawnd here."

Bulps: Onion-shaped objects. "It's dark in here. You need new light bulps."

Bumper: A flying machine used to drop explosive devices called bumps. "My friend Steve served in the 99th Bumper Diwision in the Air Force."

Bunnit: A woman's hat. "Sadie wears her bunnit every Easter only now."

Bush: A shove. "Can you give me a bush? I need to get my car started."

Bus: To make a whiny noise. "Does the bussing of bees in your ear bother you?"

C

Cap: A commercial vehicle. "Do you take the bus or do you take a cap?"

Caw: A bovine animal. "Sarah still milks her caw by hand."

Cello: A type of food. "I like a good strawberry cello for dessert."

Cheap: A type of vehicle. "To get to our cabin we have to drive a cheap."

Cheneration of Wipers: A group of wicked people who are all about the same age. "Our preacher warned us about the dangers of becoming a cheneration of wipers."

"Get out the buck spray!"

Gary Gates

Chermins: People from Cherminy. "Most of our forefathers in this area were Chermins."

Cherry: A man's name. "My favorite comedian is Cherry Lewis."

Choke: A funny story. "It's an art to deliver a good choke."

Chop: An occupation. "All he needs to get going in life is a good chop."

Choy: An elated feeling. "My family fills me with choy."

Chuck: A container used to hold liquids. "We like to get together and share a frosty chuck of birch beer on hot summer days."

Chuckler Wayne: A major blood vessel. "Can you feel the chuckler wayne in your neck?"

Chump: To leap. "Don't chump in before you know what you're getting into."

Chunk: Garbage, refuse. "Some people think modern art is just a lot of chunk."

Chust: Only. "Chust a little more pie, please."

Clod: White puffs of water vapor in the air. "I wandered, lonely as a clod."

Close: What we wear. "Katie is washing her close in the sink."

Clup: An exclusive group. "Groucho Marx wouldn't join any clup that would have him as a member."

Collitch: An institution of higher learning. "I can speak so much better since I went to collitch."

Colt: Opposite of hot. "I like the colt because I'm a skier."

Crick: A tributary to a river. "We caught some crayfish in the crick."

Crip: What a baby sleeps in. "We put the baby in the crip every night at eight o'clock."

Crod: A large group of people. "What a crod! Everybody in town must've come!"

Crutch: To hold a bad opinion of; resentment. "Nick holds a crutch against Ben and won't go with him anywhere."

Crotch: A building in which cars are kept. "My husband is working over in Amos' crotch helping him to fix a flat tire."

Cummin Sense: What everybody knows. "Why, it's only cummin sense you don't do it like that!"

Cun: To deceive. "That shyster's trying to cun you out of your money."

Cunked Awt: To give awt; to break dawn. "My car cunked awt on me last night and I had to walk twenty miles home."

Cuntack: A connection; also a small optical lense. "Bill's cuntack popped awt when he was playing basketball last night."

"For such a big crotch he sure has a small wehicle."

The Complete Book of Dutch-ified English

Cuppert: A kitchen cabinet. "After you dry the dishes, stack them in the cuppert."

Cussin: A relative. "My cussin is fun to play with."

D

Damitch: Hurt or harm. "The damitch to the barn from fire was extensive."

Also: "He's going to sue for damitches."

Dasselt: To have impressed mightily. "Houdini dasselt the audiences with his daring escapes."

Dairsent: Not allowed to. "I dairsent smoke in school."

Dawn: The opposite of up. "Dawn by the river where the britch meets is where Harry fishes."

Debt: Deceased. "Barbara's been amonk the debt for some time."

Dents: Places where lions live and men brood. "Harold has so much stuff, he has two dents in the hawse."

Dewide: To distribute, apportion. "Be sure you dewide the candy equally between the children or they'll be sure to fuss."

Also a boundary that splits something in two.

"Last summer ve drove over the Continental Dewide."

Dick: To bore into the earth. "When did Scott dick his well?"

Also to investigate. "I'm going to dick into that mystery and find awt."

Dippy Eck: An eck fried sunnyside up. (See **Eck**).

Dissy: Off balance. "When I climb too high I get dissy."

Also: "Dissy Dean was a great baseball player."

Donut: Ain't. "This cake sure eats good, donut?"

Dootle: Draw aimlessly. "You can't just dootle in life if you want to make a work of art."

Doppick: Dumb; not too smart. "Chester is so doppick he can't barely run his car, much less a farm."

Dotch: A make of car. "Fannie loves her new black Dotch, it rides so fine."

Drainitch: What takes the water off. "This drainitch system doesn't work so awful good. Ve need new pipes."

Dretch: Low life. "Ve must help lift people out of the dretches of existence."

Drife: To pilot a car. "Do you want to drife?"

Duck: Past tense of dick. "Is the well duck yet?"

Dunnult: A man's name. "Dunnult Duck is my son's favorite cartoon."

Dupple: Two of. "Twins are dupple people."

Burying the debt.

E

Eck: What a hen lays. "Dip your toast in the dippy eck to see what good is!"

Eck Nock: A Christmas drink made with milk, eck, and rum. "Pop's eck nock tastes wonderful good!"

Etchicated: To be well learnt. "I want my daughter to be better etchicated than I am, that's for sure."

Eefning: After afternoon and before night. "The sunset glowed pretty and gave us a beautiful eefning."

Effry: All of them; each one. "Ve eat a good breakfast effry morning."

Enchineer: A person who drives a train. "As kids, ve'd vave to get the enchineer to blast the vhistle for us."

Erased: A man who drives too fast. "Erased a car in the Grand Prix!"

Erector: To have demolished something. "You know Chakie's new car? Erector!"

Et: To have eaten. "Chunny's et himself full already for the night."

Etch: A border or boundary. "Some people thought Columbus would sail over the etch of the world."

Ewade: Avoid. "Don't try to ewade the issue."

F

Faar: Combustion; flames. "Vhere there's smoke, there's faar."

Face: Belief; religious conwiction. "Praise be! Rebecca has found her face in the Lord again!"

False: What water does. "Ve honeymooned at Niagra False."

Famly: A related group of people. "Without a famly, I'd be nothing."

Fausnacht: A donut. "Sarah dunks a fausnacht in her coffee in the morning."

Fergib: To pardon, excuse. "Ve must fergib those who trespass against us."

Ferginny: An American state. "Chorch Washington was born in Ferginny."

Ferhoodle: To perplex, puzzle. "Calculus class sure ferhoodles me."

Fife: One more than four. "There are fife days in a work week."

File: Poultry. "Turkeys sure are an ugly looking file."

Also unpleasant, putrid: "Vhat is that file odor?"

Fill: To touch. "Let me fill your silky hair."

Filling: What everybody else calls stuffing. "Do you

prefer sausage or potato filling in the turkey at Thanksgiving?"

Finker: A digit on your hand. "If you buy your sweetheart a ring, make sure it fits her finker."

Fiss: What carbonated drinks do. "Vhen you put ice cream in a Coke, it really fisses, ain't?"

Fix: Cook. "Honey, can you fix me some eggs? I haf to eat and run quick."

Flar: Grawnd wheat used in baking. "Add two cups of flar to the batter and it'll thicken up good."

Flack: What flies on a flackpole. "Don't you get a lump in your throat vhenever you salute the flack?"

Fond: To have discovered. "I'm glad Columbus fond America instead of China. Othervise, I don't know vhere I'd be living."

For So: For the fun of it. "Do you vant to go steady, or chust for so?"

Frawn: A negative facial expression. "Vhy do some people frawn at us, Pop?"

Futch: A type of candy or chocolate sauce. "I like my hot futch sundaes with a cherry on top."

G

Garbitch: Refuse; junk. "I hate taking out the garbitch."

Garklin: Rinsing the back of your throat with mouthwash. "Ve always hear our Dad garklin in the morning."

Get Awt: An expression of surprise. "Get awt! I never said that!"

Gluff: An article of clothing worn on the hand to protect it. "I always vear rupper gluffs to do the dishes."

Gookamoedoe: Look at that. "Gookamoedoe! Zachariah and Amy are giving each other the eye!"

Goot: The opposite of bad. "I love to curl up with a goot book."

Got: The divine being. "I thank Got for all I have."

Go To: Take to something. "If your children go to books, you'd better be quick for some good questions."

Grackers: Unleavened bread. "Graham grackers are great, but not in soup."

Graiffy: Sauce from meat cookings. "Do you like graiffy bread?"

Graadiate: To earn an academic degree or diploma. "Sadie did real good in her studies and she's going to graadiate from Kutztawn State Collitch next week."

Grawch: Someone who gripes. "Don't let him get you dawn, he's chust an old grawch."

Grawnd: Earth, soil. "Lankister Cawnty has some of the best grawnd in the world for growing things."

Grex: To complain; moan. "Ah, quit your grexing, you have a vonderful life."

Grum: The guy who marries the bride. "I was only a grum one time, and that was enough."

Gruntbecky: An expression of hard going. "Gruntbecky! It's difficult to run in this hot sun."

Gunked Up: To smear grease on. "If you get those ball bearings gunked up your bike'll run smoother."

H

H: Number of years a person or a thing has. "Vhat's your H?"
Also: "Mattie, is this cheese properly H'd?"

Hank: Dangle; suspend. "Vhere should I hank my coat?"

Har: A terrible disgust or fright. "Har movies are scary."

Hawse: Where Pennsylwania Dutchmen dwell. "Come on over to our hawse."

Also a question: "Hawse the weather today?"

Haw: In what manner or way. "Haw much do you want for this?"

Heart: Not easy. "Emma's got a heart life."

Heef: To forcefully throw. "Heef this ballast over the side to lighten the ship."

Heel: Elevated ground; a knoll. "Daniel ran up that heel without stopping?"

Heffen: Where you go if you're good. "Vill I be seeing you in heffen?"

Height: Conceal. "Vhere can you height an elephant?"

Herititch: Tradition. "Our American herititch is amacing."

Het: The round thing on top of your neck. "If you don't use your het to get ahet, you're bond to fail."

Hex Sign: A rawnd sign with a pretty design meant to scare away the devil and make a barn look pretty. "Josh's barn got a new hex sign yet."

Hock: A large swine. "Levi gets good pork from his hocks."

Hoppy: A recreation activity. "Do you have any hoppies? My hoppy's coin collecting."

Huck: An affectionate squeeze. "Come and give your aunt a big huck!"

Hun: A sweetheart. "I'm going to the concert tonight with my hun."

Hunert: Ten tens. "I hope to live to be a hunert."

Hunk: Past tense of hank. "He was hunk for his crimes."

Hunkry: Famished; starved. "I'm so hunkry I could eat a horse."

Hurrieder: Faster. "The hurrieder I go, the behinder I get."

I

Ice: What you see with. "Craig has green ice in his head."

Also: "My, what pretty ice you have!"

Imitch: A projection, shadow, or replica of. "He's going to have to project a better imitch if he wants this chop."

Immejitly: Right away. "Aaron! You stop kicking her immejitly!"

In: At the place of. "He turns the gate in to get to the store."

Indiwisiple: Not dewisiple. "This nation is one nation, indiwisiple."

Indiwitchally: By oneself. "They drove indiwitchally."

Infectious: A woman who is indeed doing something. "Is she in school? Vhy sure, infectious working on her doctorate yet."

Injun: A motor. "You'll need a good mechanic to fix your injun."

Inklish: A lankwitch, or a person from Inkland. "His Inklish isn't so good."

Innilect: Brains. "Einstein was a man of high innilect."

Innockilate: Vaccinate. "The kids get innockilated in school."

Intellichintz: Brains. "An IQ test tests your intellichintz."

Inntrest: Money earned on a loan. "My bank pays good inntrest."

Inwade: To attack a place to occupy it. "It was a mistake for Napoleon to inwade Russia."

Inwaluble: Priceless. "A painting by Wan Go is inwaluble."

Inwariable: Not warying. "The speed of light is inwariable in any medium."

Inwent: Create. "Inwent a perpetual-motion machine? I'm too tired."

Investigate: Look into; explore. "Man is meant to inwestigate the heavens."

Inwhite: Ask over. "Did you inwhite the Smiths for supper?"

Inwolve: To include; to make a part of. "I don't vant to get inwolved."

Iragoy: An Indian tribe. "The Iragoy were a north voods people."

J

Jap: Punch. "Kevin threw a jap at me when I told him what I thought of him."

Japder: A division of a book. "The hero rescues the maiden in japder nine."

Jams: Night close. "Go put on your jams, it's time to go to bet."

Jewelery: Adornments for the body. "Even men wear jewelery these days."

Jinkle: The sound small bells make. "Jinkle bells! Jinkle bells! Jinkle all da vay!"

Jock: To run slowly. "There's nothing like a good jock to keep you in shape."

Jutch: Criticize. "Jutch not that you be not jutched."

Wan Go: See definition of "Inwaluble."

K

Keel: Slay. "If I would have had a gun the other day, I could have keeled a deer."

Also: "Thou shalt not keel."

Ken: To be able to. "Ken you run the mile in six minutes? Kenny ken!"

Kenya: Are you able. "Kenya come?"

Ketch: To grasp. "Did you ketch what that eckhead said?"

Also: "Let's go awtside and ketch ball."

Also: "You'll ketch it if your Mom finds awt."

Kilt: To have keeled. "Carl kilt a bear last hunting season."

Kink: The ruler of a country. "Prince Charles will someday become the next Kink of Inkland."

Kits: Children. "How many kits do you have? I have four kits, and they drife me crazy!"

Knack: An old horse. "Did you buy that knack at the auction?"

Also to pester or harass: "All my vife does is knack when I'm home."

Knowed: To have the acquaintance of. "Did you think you knowed me?"

Kumpis: An instrument that tells direction. "If you

Last year Run kilt a bear.

go alone into the vilderness, take a kumpis with you."

Kumpny: Wisitors. "We're having kumpny over for supper tonight."

L

Lacy: Not active. "Tom is so lacy, he got a goat to mow his lawn."

Lankister Cawnty: The heartland of Pennsylwania Dutch country, commonly misspelled on maps as "Lancaster County." "I wish they all could be Lankister Cawnty girls."

Lankwitch: A system of speech. "I still can't make awt what fer lankwitch he uses yet."

Larch: Not small. "That's a larch tree."
"No, that's an oak."
"I know, it's a larch oak."

Lasty: Durable, long-lasting. "Bluecheens are wery lasty trawsers."

Lawd: High wolume sawnd. "For cryin' awt lawd, you shoulda known better."

Launch: To relax. "Pop likes to launch in his easy chair at night."

Leaf: To go away or to be gone. "Leaf me alone!"

A rupdawn is good for a missreple kink.

Learnt: To have grasped a supject. "I sure learnt a lot of Inklish in high school. Did you?"

Lecks: What you walk on. "My lecks are weary from standing on market all day."

Lentz: A piece of glass used to refocus light. "His lentz popped out of his glasses."

Lepnin: A tawn in central Pennsylwania famous for the best bologna in the world. "I'm not hunkry anymore, but I sure could eat some more Lepnin boloney with ketchep on it."

   Also a country in the Mideast. "Those hichackers make Lepnin a dangerous place to wisit."

Libber: A body organ. "There's nothing like eating a good piece of libber for supper."

Liff: Dwell, survive. "Vhere do you liff? In a hawse?"

Little: A small amount of. "I only want a little." "Come over for a little."

Lochencher: A cough drop. "Suck on this lochencher for relief."

Loose: To misplace something. "Did you loose your wallet again?"

Looser: A famous Reformer. "Looser was excommunicated from the Roman Catholic Church for his ideas."

Lotch: A country cabin or a clup. "Pete likes to go to the lotch with the boys whenever he ken."

Mom and Pop like to launch arawnd on Sunday afternoon.

Also to stay with. "Why not lotch with us tonight?"

Luckitch: Bagitch; a collection of suitcases. "Does effrything you need to travel fit in your luckitch?"

Luff: The greatest feeling in the world. "Fill your heart with luff!"

Also what people fall in. "Mary and Isaac are in luff."

Lunks: What your breathe with. "You need big lunks on you to swim underwater for more than two minutes."

M

Make: An all purpose word for action. "Make the window shut." "Make the dirt away." "The doorbell don't make."

Make Awt: To turn off. "Make awt the light. I want to sleep!"

Also to turn on: "Esther and Bill were making awt and got so excited they missed the bus."

Make Dawn: To rain. "Take your umbrella, it's making dawn awtside."

Mal: 5,280 feet. "I'd walk a million mals, for one of

your smals . . ."

Manitch: To run in an organized manner. "You have to learn how to manitch yourself before you can manitch others."

Manury: Full of natural fertilizer. "That scheme is manury."

Maple: A woman's name. "Maple luffs Cherry."

Maritch: Matrimony. "Maritch can be a lot of hard work."

Mate: Constructed, built. "Rose mate this quilt with her own hands."

Mawntins: Larch hills covered with trees. "Ve haff a cabin in the mawntins for wacation."

Mawse: A small rodent. "A mawse lives in our bedroom wall."

Mawth: What food goes into and sawnd comes awt of. "Ach, shut your mawth!"

Maychur: A military rank. "Richard's a maychur in the Green Berets."

McDunultz: A fast food chain. "Ve take the famly to McDunultz for Bic Macs."

Meal: A place where grain is crushed. "They mate a restrent awt of the olt meal dawn by the stream."

Meppy: Perhaps. "Meppy I will, and meppy I won't."

Missreple: Unhappy, uncomfortable. "Stop being so missreple."

Mohegans: An Indian tribe. "James Fennimore Cooper wrote "The Last of the Mohegans."

Moof: Relocate. "I hate to moof."

Moofies: Films. "People like to eat popcorn when they go to the moofies."

Morkitch: A loan on a hawse. "Six more payments and my morkitch is all!"

Muck: A large cup. "A muck of coffee gets you going in the morning."

Mutt: Wet grawnd. "Children luff to play in the mutt. That's not too bat, but you have to mind they don't eat mutt pies yet."

N

Nalentz: Ladies' hosiery. "Excuse me, but there's a runner in your nalentz."

Nassaress: The town where Jesus grew up. "Nassaress is in the Holy Land yet."

Natchral: Normal, not artificial. "It's only natchral to speak dis vay."

Naw: An expression of disbelief. "Naw come on!" Also, right away: "I want it done naw."

Needer: Not one or the other. "Needer one of them will budge."

Nerf: A neuron that controls the movements of muscles. "You have to have good nerfs to be a surgeon."

Nix Nootz: A devilish, mischievious person. "Our daughter is a little nix nootz."

No: Any. "I don't got no melons today."

Noah: Used to emphasize the negative. "Did I do it? Noah!"

Nohaw: No way. "This relationship's no good nohaw."

Noiss: Sawnd. "What's that noiss?"

Nootles: What Pennsylwania Dutchmen eat when other people are eating pasta. "Eck nootles make a body full."

Noose: Current events. "I watch the CBS noose effry night. Sometimes that daily noose gets depressing. But I always read *The Lepnin Daily Noose*."

Nootzer: A big marble. "One nootzer is worth five smaller marbles."

Norse: A direction opposite of souse. "Santa Claus lives at the Norse Pole."

Nowember: The eleventh month. "Hunting season starts in Nowember."

Nun: The total lack of; zero. "After Linda ate the last apple, we had nun."

Nutzed Up: Messed up. "The President's got the budget all nutzed up."

Nutzin' Arawnd: Goofing arawnd; fooling arawnd. "If you don't have anything better to do, you often end up chust nutzin' arawnd."

O

Oafer: Above. "Somewhere, oafer the rainbow . . ."

Odder: An aquatic animal. "Odders sure are playful in the water."

Off: Wacation time. "My off is all until next year." Also no trespassing: "Keep the grass off!"

Olt: The opposite of yunk. "Ve grow too soon olt, and too late smart."

Opchect: A thing, a point. "Vhat's the opchect of this lesson?"

Oranch: A fruit from Florida. "Oranch choose is best for breakfast."

Ott: Unusual. "Some people sure speak ott."

Ouches: Hurts, pains. "This cut ouches me so."

Outen: To turn off; extinguish. "Outen the light, I want to go to sleep."

P

Pawder: Talcum. "Vhat's the vite stuff on your neck? Vhy, it's pawder!"

Pal: A heap; a stack. "Put that wood in a pal so it doesn't take up the whole yard yet."
   Also: "Make a pal with those boxes."

Packitch: A parcel. "Take these packitches over to your Aunt Martha's."

Paitch: What this is written on. "Turn the paitch when you're finished for more."

Par: Force, energy. "He is a man of great par."
   Also: "Does your car have par steering?"

Pawt: To frawn; to brood. "He pawts when he doesn't get his own vay."

Peace: Green things that come in a pod. "You must eat your peace before you get dessert."

Peck: A short wooden rod. "Hang your coat on the peck."

Peel: A medicinal tablet. "Swallow your peels and you'll feel better."

Peep peeps: Baby chickens. "Kids love to get peep peeps for Easter."

Pennsylwania: A state of the Union commonly mis-spelled as "Pennsylvania." "Come to Pennsylwania and enchoy yourself."

Pick: A small swine. "Do you make bacon from your butchered picks?"

Pichur: A photograph. "Who's that lady in the pichur?"

Plah: To put furrows in a field. "Ezekiel still uses horses to plah with."

Pleece: The magic word. "May I pleece have some more ice cream, Mom?"

Pletch: To give an oath. "Do they say the Pletch of Allechance in school anymore?"

Prod: To take pleasure in something. "Most people are prod to be Americans."

Powvower: A folk medicine healer. "A powvower cured my mom from scarlet fever when she was a beppy."

Precedent: The man in charge. "A Dutchman would be a good precedent."

Produse: Foodstuffs. "Farmer's market has the freshest produse."

Prum: A high school dance. "Bill's taking Sue to the prum this year."

Prumiss: To pledge; swear. "Do you prumiss to love her til death do you part?"

Punnyack: A make of car. "A chief vas the hood ornament on a Punnyack."

Pup: An English bar. "In London, we drank some beer in a pup."

Purse: A cat's murmur. "She's soothed by the kitten's purse."

Q

Quiss: A quickie exam. "Did you pass that last quiss in class?"

R

Rawnd: Circular. "Columbus thought the world was rawnd before most people."

Receipt: A list of ingredients in a particular food. "May I have the receipt for this delicious shoo-fly pie?"

Reckler: Ordinary. "He's chust a reckler fellow."

Red: To clean or straighten up. "Red up your room before kumpny comes."

Restrent: A place where people eat out. "That restrent has home cooking!"

Rhett: A primary color. "The new firetruck is rhett."

Donnult lets out Grandma's secret receipt.

Rhum: Part of a house. "Go to your rhum and stay there till I say!"

Rice: Comes up. "Where does the sun rice?"

Rick: Equip, prepare. "Ken you rick my yacht for a rawnd-the-world trip?"

Rink: A rawnd metal band worn on a finger. "Cyrus gave Velma a rink for Christmas."

Rips: Bones that cover the lunks. "Don't tickle me in the rips!"

Ritch: A mawntin range. "From up on that ritch you ken see twenty mals."

Rocket: To shake something back and forth. "If you want to stay safe in a canoe, don't rocket."

Romanic: Passionate; in a loving, appreciative mood. "Lord Byron was a romanic poet."

Rot: A wooden staff. "Choe borrowed my fishing rot."

Ruck: Soft material that covers a floor. "Wipe your shoes on that ruck."

Ruint: Spoiled. "Those steaks were ruint when you burnt them."

Rummitch sale: A sale of used stuff. "He's so cheap he buys his close at rummitch sales."

Run: A man's name. "Pop, is Reagan's first name Run?"

Rupdawn: A massage. "A goot rupdawn will take

the ache away."

Rupper: A polymer of isoprene. "Rupper boots will keep your feet dry."

Ruse: A woman's name. "My mom likes to read abawt Ruse in the Bible."

Rutch: To squirm. "Ted! Stop rutching in the pew and listen to the sermon."

Ruts: A famly's heritich. "Our ruts go back to Cherminy."

Also the part of a plant that holds it in the grawnd: "A man is like a plant. If he doesn't put dawn ruts someplace, he'll never grow."

Ruff: The top of a hause. "His ruff leaks."

S

Safe: To put money in a bank account. "The Japanese safe more than we do."

Sale: To offer something for sale. "Are you going to sale your hawse?"

Sar: Not sweet. "A sweet goes goot with a sar."

Satellite: A term coined by the Pennslwania Dutch. "Chake and Amos were awt in the fields one night when the unusual brightness of the newly launched Sputnik flew overhead. Chake said, 'Hey, Amos, satellite?' "

Sawnd: Vibrations in the air. "You hear that sawnd? Sawnds like a bird."

Scar: Scrub with cleanser. "Richard! Go scar the tub!"

Schmutz: To gunk up. "Schmutz up that axle with grease and it'll run better."

Shar: Precipitation. "April shars bring May flars."

Shooker: Sucrose. "Don't use too much shooker in that cake yet."

Shooker Scoop: The bonnet that plain women wear. "Esther looks goot in her new shooker scoop."

Shtamp: Something put on an envelope so the Post Office will mail it. "Give me a shtamp for this letter, please."

Shuffle: A tool, or the act of using that tool. "I like to shuffle the walks whenever it snows."

Shushly: Always bissy; fidgeting. "She's too shushly to chust sit and talk."

Sick and sin: Rough times. "She saw her diet through sick and sin."

Sick sack: Weave back and forth. "A skier knows haw to sick sack."

Sink: Cogitate. "Use your head to sink a little." Also to make music with your woice: "Our choir

Sinking classical music.

prefers to sink classical music."

Site: Location. "Iss it on the right site or the left site of the road?"

Sitiate: To place; arrange. "We chust got here and we're not sitiated yet."

Slippy: A surface on which something can slide. "Walk carefully, it's slippy as a banana peel."

Smooch: Kiss. "Smooch me on the lips, you little darling."

Snack: Catch. "Did you see him snack that fly ball?"

Somesing: A particular thing. "It makes somesing dawn like a drissle."

Sop: To cry. "She softly sopped herself to sleep."

Souse: The opposite of norse. "Pam lives on the souse side of town."

Speck: Fat. "Meat with too much speck in it is heart to chew."

Spritz: Sprinkle with water. "Our Pop used to spritz us with the hose when it got too hot in the summer."

Statue: Asked of someone to determine their identity. "Hey Pete, statue?"

Still: Do it yet. "She didn't still."

Strife: Struggle. "You must strife to succeed."

Strubly: Disheveled, unkempt. "Run a comb through your strubly hair wunst."

Superwise: To direct. "Who will superwise the prochect?"

Surf: To perform an obligation. "Did you surf a big meal to your kumpny?"

T

Taar: A round piece of rubber. "The car's taars are worn out."

Tack: The art of gentle persuasion. "If you want to motivate people, you have to use a great deal of tack."

Tame people: Good people. "If tame people would leaf government to the rowdies, how would it be?"

Tar: A high structure. "When I think of Paris, I think of the Eiffel Tar."

Tawn: A small city. "I'm going to the farmer's market in tawn."

Tawsin: Ten hunerts. "It's a tawsin to one against."

Tee wee: What everybody watches. "What shows are on Tee Wee tonight?"

Telewishin: Tee Wee. "Telewishin can be an etchicational tool."

Themselfs: Those very people. "Do you think they can handle it themselfs?"

Think: An object. "What is that? I never saw a think like that before."

Thirsty: The day before Fridy. "My birthday's Thirsty."

Thistle: It'll. "Thistle do the trick."

Throttle: Spank. "Your Dad's gonna throttle you when he gets home!"

Tile: An absorbent cloth. "Rub this tile on your face and get the dirt off."

To bank: To go where the money's kept. "Why, I chust went to bank."

Togedder: Both at once. "They're going togedder."

Toiss: Playthings. "Mom! Sara's playing with my toiss again!"

Tomar: The day after today. "Tomar is another day."

Tooah: Also. "Chennie's coming tooah."

Toose: An exposed bone in the mouth used for chewing. "Isaiah lost his toose in a fight."

Toosedy: The day after Mondy. "If this is Toosedy, it must be Belgium."

Track: A parcel of land. "Are you going to build on that track of land?"

Trafel: Roam; explore. "You ken trafel through time in a good book."

Tricker: Part of a gun. "For best results don't pull the tricker; squeeze the tricker."

Trupple: Problems; no good. "His son's always in trupple."

Tuck: Pull. "Tuck the rope when you reach the bottom of the heel."

Tuck boat: A type of boat. "The tuck boats pushed the Queen Mary into the open sea."

Tum: A man's name. "Tum Sawyer is a classic."

Tum-tum: An Indian drum. "The Sioux dance to the beat of a tum-tum."

Tup: Where you bathe. "Lettie slipped in the tup and broke her hip."

Turiss: A trafler. "Did you buy this book as a turiss, or not?"

U

Udder: Something else. "I always try to look at the udder side of things."

Ukly: Terrible looking; horrible. "War is ukly."

Um: Those people or things. "Don't look at me; I don't have um."

Unner: Integrity. "On my unner, I will do my best."

Also a judge: "But Your Unner, I didn't mean to do it, unnest!"

Up: Where things get done; a general word used to help make the meaning of a sentence clear. "Clean up your plate."

"Go up to the counter and order up."

"Eat up! There's plenty more coming up!"

V

Ve: More than one of us. "Are ve going to the show?"

Vase: A piece; a little bit. "It's chust up the road a vase."

Vault: A man's name. "You ken always take your kits to see a Vault Disney moofie."

Vawtch: Look at. "Vawtch the stars at night and catch a glimpse of heffen."

Vear: To clothe. "I don't know what I'll vear on her."

Veddink: A matrimonial ceremony. "Did you get a gift for their veddink yet?"

Veed: A pest plant. "Dandelion is a veed, but we eat it yet."

Vell: A place where water is drawn. "Throw a coin in the vishing vell."

Ven: A question. "Ven is leap year next?"

Vent: Gone. "I don't know vhere the time vent!"

Verk: Labor; function. "Tum verks in a store."

Verlt var von: A big conflict. "Verlt Var Von started Verlt Var Two."

Verse: Not as good as; deteriorating. "Naomi's colt is getting verse."

Vet: Not dry. "That vet awtside will give you a cold if you don't bundle up."

Vice: Intelligent. "Benjamin Franklin was a vice man."

Vidda: A woman who has lost her husband through death.

  Also, a well-known spider: "The black vidda is dangerous."

Vhy: Question the reason for. "Vhy must we fight? Vhy not peace wunst?"

Vile: During; a moment. "Come on, sit dawn and stay for a vile."

Vill: Concentration. "You can do anything if you have the vill."

Vin: Achieve victory. "Who will vin the lottery?"

Vine: Fermented grape chooce. "Chester drank all the vine."

Viper: Scrapers on a vindshield. "My vindshield vipers are screeching."

Vhistle: A shrill sawnd. "If you need me, chust vhistle."

Vood: Tree flesh. "He's a vould-be voodverker."

Vootz: A bunch of trees. "The vootz are full of animals."

Vulfes: Wild dogs. "The vulfes attacked the caribou."

W

Wacuum: Emptiness. "Nature abhors a wacuum." Also short for a wacuum cleaner: "When you're finished dusting, you ken wacuum."

Wack: Move back and forth. "My dog wacks its tail vhenever it sees me."

Walley: A space between mawntins. "Dawn in the walley, the walley so low . . ."

Walyue: Worth; the sum of. "To get the ratio, dewide walyue one by walyue two."

Wanilla: A flavor. "Wanilla ice cream is great!"

Wary: Fluctuate. "Do you wary your routine?"

Wassleen: Petroleum jelly. "Smear wassleen on a beppy's bottom vhen it sore gets."

Wayne: Futile, to no awail. "Nick's attempt to climb the mawntin was in wayne."

Wechtapels: Carrots, peas, and such. "Our famly eats a wechtapel effry day."

Wee C.R.: A Tee Wee taping machine. "Our Wee C.R. is handy."

Wee I.P.: A big shot. "Wee I.P.s always drive in limousines."

Wee W: A make of car. "Doris has two Wee W's: a Buck and a Wan."

Wehicle: A car, truck, etc. "Is that your wehicle parked awtside?"

Went: An opening for circulation. "It was sucked in the air went."

Wery: A great deal. "Thank you wery much."

Wet: Short for wetern. "He's a Wietnam wet."
   Also short for weternarian: "Your caw's sick; better call the wet."

Wice: Deputy. "What does the wice-president do, exactly?"

Wideo: Tee Wee moofies on tapes. "Do you make home wideos?"

Wifes: Maritch partners. "A bigamist has two wifes."

Wilentz: Extreme aggression. "Wilentz begets wilentz."

Willitch: A small tawn. "In the willitch by the stream lived a maiden fair."

"Go ahead, eat yourself full. You can jock it off tomar!"

Wim And Wicker: Energy. "She was so full of wim and wicker in her youth."

Wine: A long plant. "Grapes grow on wines, you dummy."

Wisit: Socialize. "Stay and wisit wunst."

With: Along. "Are you coming with?"

Also a general purpose word used to end a sentence. "This newspaper is wery good to line a cupboard with."

Wolwo: A Swedish car. "My Wolwo never lets me dawn."

Wootzer: A little pig. "Vhy you little wootzer!"

Wonders: Amazes; perplexes. "Life wonders me so."

Woted: Cast a ballot. "Haw many people woted in the last election?"

Wow: Swear; promise. "Alden and Martha exchanged wedding wows last Saturday night."

Wrench: To run water over to get the soap off. "Wrench the dishes after you wash them."

Wunst: One time. "Spread me wunst over with butter a piece of bread."

Also at a certain time. "Wunst upon a time, on a dark and stormy night . . ."

Wurst: The opposite of best. "That's the wurst show I've ever seen."

Also chopped liver. "That wurst is the best I've eaten."

X

X: Plural of eck. "Do you eat X for breakfast?"

Y

Yet: Used to end a sentence in a general way. "Is supper ready yet?" "Chakie went to the store yet." "Is it raining yet?"

Yous: Used to distinguish the plural of you. "Are yous coming with, or are chust you coming with?"

Yunk: Not olt. "The yunk ones today sure are different."

Z

Zent: A penny. "Who asked for your two zents?"

Zinc: What you wash dishes in. "Put the dishes in the zinc."

Zoop: A hot, liquid meal. "Is it zoop yet?"

For Reading Awt Lawd

In the following passages, the influence of Dutchified English is profound. They are designed to be read out loud. Some of the texts are familiar ones, so if a meaning isn't clear, look up the Standard English version. Most of the words used are not listed in the Dictionary part of this book, but by now you likely are ready for a journey into uncharted terrain, ready to make new discoveries.

Ape Lincoln's Geddysburk Address

Fourscore ent sefen yearse ago our fodders brawght forth on dis cuntinent a new nation, cunseeft in liperty, and deddicated to de proposition dat all men are crated equal.

Naw ve are engaitched in a crate ciffil var, testing vedder dat nation or enny nation so cunseeft and so deddicated ken lonk endure. Ve are met on a crate baddle feelt uff dat var. Ve haff kum to deddicate a portion uff dat feelt, aas a final rest in place fer dose who here gafe dare lifes dat dat nation might liff. It iss altogedder fittin and proper dat ve shoult do dis.

But, in a larcher sense, ve ken not deddicate, ve ken not cunsecrate, ve ken not hollow dis grawnd. Dese brafe men, liffing ent debt, who strukkled here, haff cunsecrated it, far abofe are poor par to at or detrack. Da verlt vill liddle note, nor lonk re-

Ape Lincoln

memper vhat ve say here, but it ken nefer fergit vhat day dit here. It iss fer us, da liffing, radder, to be deddicated to de unfinshed verk vhich day who fought here haff dus far so noply adwanced. It is radder fer us to be here deddicated to de crate task remainin bafore us—dat frum dese unnert debt ve take increased dewotion to dat causs for vhich dey gafe de lass full messher uff dewotion—dat ve here highly resolfe dat dese debt shall not haff dite in wayne—dat dis nation, unner Got, shall haff a new birth uff freedim—ent dat guffernmint uff da peeple, by da peeple, fer da peeple, shall not perish frum da earse.

Pletch Uff Allechintz to de Flack

I pletch allechintz to de flack uff de Unided States uff America ent to de repuplic fer vhich it stance, von nation unner Got, indiwisiple, viss liperty ent chustice fer all.

A Slection Frum Chulus Ceaser, Act Schree, Scene Twoah
Antnee's Speech to da Roamints

Frents, Roamints, Cuntrymen, Lent me your earce,
I kum to burry Ceaser, not to prase him,
De efil dat men do liffs afder dem;
De goot iss oft interrd viss dare bontz.
So led it be viss Ceaser. De nople Brudis
Hass tolt ya Ceaser vass ambitious;
Iff it ver so, it vass a griefiss fault.
Ent griefissly hass Ceaser answerdt it.
Here, unner leaf uff Brudus ent da rest,
Fer Brudis iss a hunraple man;
So dey all, all hunraple men,
Kum I ta speak inn Ceaser's funral.

First Curinsins, Chatter Sirteen, Werse Von to Sirteen.

Doe I speak wiss da tunks uff anchals, ent haff not luff, I am bekum aas sawndin brass, or a tinklin simple.

2. Ent doe I haff da giff uff proffcy, ent unnerstant all mistries, ent all knowletch, ent doe I haff face, so dat I couldt remoofe mawntins, ent haff not luff, I am nodding.

3. Ent doe I bestow all my goots to feed da pore, ent doe I giff my buddy to be burnt, ent haff not luff, it profiss me nodding.

4. Luff sufferse lonk, ent iss kindt; luff enwies not; luff vants not itselve, iss not puffed up.

5. Dust not behafe itselve unseemly, seeks not her own, iss not easely prawoked, sinks no efil.

6. Rechoyce not in niquity, but rechoyce in da truce.

7. Baress all tinks, beleafs all tinks, hopes all tinks, enduress all tinks.

8. Luff nefer failse: bud wedder dare be proffcies, dey shall fail, wedder dare be tunks, dey shall cease; wedder dare be knowletch, it shall wanish avay.

9. Fer ve knowse in part, en ve proffcy in part.

10. But ven dat vhich iss purrfict iss kum, den

dat vhich iss inn part shall be dun avay.

11. Ven I vass a childt, I spaked aas a childt, I unnerstoot aas a childt, I taught aas a childt: but ven I became a mann, I pud avay childtish sings.

12. Fer naw ve see thru a glass darkly; but den face to face, naw I noah in part, but den I shall noah efen aas also I am noan.

13. Ent naw abites face, hope, luff, dese shree, but da cratist of dese iss luff.

Haw to Haff A Goot Rummitch Sell at Your Hawse

Von: Gadder up all your olt chunk.

Twoah: Place an at in da noose paper.

Schree: Put sighnts in your yart.

Four: Vait fer buyerse to kum, ent sale dem at a goot price.

Fife: Iff it makes dawn, moofe effrysing into your crotch.

On Walyuse

You know vhat walyuse are, at least I hope you haff sum.

Mathmythins sink dat a walyue iss derifed frum dewiding walyue von into walyue two ta get walyue schree.

Dat chust ain't an at up to me, doe. My walyuse are rutted in famly, home ent church. Ent ya chust can't dewide dem. It's a whole vay uff liffin.

Naw, let's consiter ecnomic walyuse. Dutchmen are known ta be tight viss a buck, but da truce iss dat day chust know da walyue uff a buck. Vasteful peeple call frookkle peeple tight, cuss dare chelliss. Dutchmen pay cash, ent so oafer da lonk run, day haff more cuss day don't pay inntrest. Besites, ta borraw only ats ta yer sorraw.

Chust look at da farm crisiss wunst. Dutchmen don't haff enny farm crisiss. Vhy? Walyuse. Day recycle. Day uus olt tinks ven dell do, ent day don't expensife fertlizers use enny, dey chust recycle da same olt manure. Day don't pollute ent day built up radder den destroy da earse yet.

Ent de Amish don't efen hafta buy fer a rainy day insurinse, cuss iff somebuddies inn trupple, like say da barn burnt dawn, day all togedder get ent raise anudder.

Ent dat's da bickest sing in walyuse—dat ve all chust reach awt ent touch each udder viss luff. Ve'd be so happy iff ve'd chust reach awt ent touch each udder, ain't?

A Dutchified Choke

Ven in kintergarten I first learnt de alphybet, I didn't get it quite right at first. I set:

ABCDEFGIKLMNOQSTUWYZ

Da teacher looked at me funny en set, "Vhy Chunny, vere's da H?"
I set, "Vhy teacher, you noah my H. It's fife."
"Den vere's da chay?"
"Aut dare, on da tree."
"Den vere's da P?"
"It's running dawn my leck."
"Ent vere's da R?"
"Up dare. On da vall. It's schree o'clock."
"Ent vere's da V?"
"Vhy teacher, V all here!"
"Ent vere's da X?"
"I hat dem fer breakfist. Dare all."

A Liddle Sumsing Extra

Haw naw brawn caw?

A Day in the Life of Johnny Huckenduppler

My name is Johnny Huckenduppler and I thought I'd try to write without an accent a day in the life of a Dutchman. I get it out a little funny sometimes, but I hope you understand.

It wonders me so how life goes. Today I was out in the field throwing the horse over the fence some hay after I had loaded the wagon off and shut the gate wide open. Amos Oberholtzer called me to the fence over to talk down a ways. We live neighbors to the Oberholtzers and our fields meet yet. They live on the hill a little up, out where the road gives a fork and then gets all.

Amos told me how he and Sarah went to Lancaster the other day and walked the town all over just to schnoz around. Amos bought some new shoes there, but he said they walked heavy so he took them back. Now it makes a body weary to hear of such dull going ons, so I told Amos I didn't have my chores caught after and I haven't the time to dopple. Amos said he could see I was already busy yet, so he told me to come down and visit them a little once some day soon. I said, "Sure, when we come the road up, we'll come over." He said, "Great, come ahead back once."

The horse was thirsty yet so I pumped myself from the well a bucket of water. My son Jacob came to sit the horse on. After he a little rode, he said, "I want down here off." Then he ran back to the house to take dinner, but on the way he ouched. I ran over to see the matter. Here he had stung his foot with a bee.

I picked him up and quick ran to the front house door. I couldn't make the door open because the lock was on. Then yet the button didn't bell, so I bumped hard the door. My wife Katie was with a vacuum sweeping the floor down, and didn't hear us. So I quick went the hind way round and got into the kitchen there. I smeared Jacob's foot all over with salve and he simmered down.

Katie ran in all ferhoodled. She looked at Jacob and said, "Ach, you look bad in the foot. You look wonderful sick. Don't you feel so good? Does it ouch you so in the foot?" She asked so many questions so fast I had to say, "Don't talk so quick—it runs together when I think."

The swelling went down as we sat ourselves awhile. Katie kissed Jacob and he said, "Mom, you're wonderful nice." She start smooching me then too, but I was hungry instead, so I said, "Kissing wears out, cooking don't."

"Well, why don't you eat yourself out more often then?" she said.

"I make the hay, you make the meals," I said. "I would rather single live than the wife the britches give."

"You ought yourself to shame," Katie said quick. "Cows come and cows go, but the bull in this house keeps coming."

She was right. I didn't want to grow too soon old and too late smart. I knew I'd better put myself other ways on. Katie learned me this, over and over.

Katie wears herself plain. But it makes me no difference. She's a good wife—she knows me yet she loves me.

We nixed our argument with a good smooch and hugged all over. I was manury from the fields yet, so upstairs I hurried and spritzed myself all over in the shower and clean became. Then I combed myself once because I was all strubbly. Katie finished redding up the house and started supper yet.

Jacob came out of his room when I was finished with myself combing. Down the stairs together we came with.

"What does it give for supper?" asked Jacob.

"I'm bad for pot pie," I said.

In the kitchen the Lebanon Bologna pot pie with heat was on the table boiling. Katie knew my hungries.

"Throw your Pop down from the cupboard some glasses," Katie said to Jacob.

I then poured us from the jug of birch beer three glasses.

Jacob drank some and said while he was still drinking, so it came out all bubbly, "This glass sure drinks wonderful good."

"Before you speak, drink your mouth empty," said Katie. "Now seat yourself down and set yourself for good eating. Supper's fixed."

I dug in too quick with hunger. The pot pie was hot and my tongue I burned. On my shirt I dropped some.

"Tuck yourself under the chin this napkin," said Katie.

I blowed the pot pie cool on my plate and wootzed it down.

"Don't eat yourself full, Pop, there's shoo-fly pie back," said Jacob.

"Well this pot pie eats so good, I must eat it all."

After we had done and Jacob went to bed, Katie looked at me and winked. "Well, the food is all but the best is yet."

We outened the lights and went up the wooden hill to the bedroom. It was making down outside and probably would continue tomorrow down.

But who cares about the rain? I thought as I climbed in the bed with Katie.

It looks for a pretty good night tonight.

To Be Sunk Awt Lawd
(For your sinking enchoyment)

O Liddle Tawn of Besselhem

O Liddle tawn of Besselhem,
Haw still ve see dee lie,
Abofe die deep ent dreamless sleep,
De silent starse go by.
Yet in de dark streets shiness
An efferlasting light,
Da hopes ent fearse uff all da yearse,
Are met in zee tonight.

Chinkle Belse

Vile dashing thru da snow
Inn a von horse open sleigh,
Oafer da feelts vill go
Laffink all da vay.
Da belse on boptail rink
Day make our spirits bright,
Vhat fun it iss to write ent sink
A sleighing sonk tonight.

Chinkle belse, chinkle belse,
Chinkle all da vay,
Oh! vhat fun it iss to write
Inn a von horse open sleigh.

Dawn in de Walley

Dawn in de walley, de walley so low,
Hank yer het oafer, hear de vint blow,
Hear de vint blow, dear, hear de vint blow,
Hank yer het oafer, hear de vint blow.

Writing dis ledder, containing schree lines,
Answer my quvestion, vill you be mine?
Vill you be mine, dear, vill you be mine?
Answer my quvestion, vill you be mine?

Roases luff sunshine, wiolets luff dew,
Anchels in heffen, know I luff you.
Know I luff you, dear, know I luff you,
Anchels in heffen, know I luff you.

Receipts
(Dese receipts really make)

Cussin Rachel's Snitz und Knepp

Ven you eat this finished, drawn in varm milk ent sprinkle on nutmeck. But cook yourself as follaws first.

Cook von pawnd bakin from a pick fer schree ares. Chently simmer von qwart sveet drite apfels viss da peel leafed on in vater smuddered. Ven da bakin iss cooked, in togedder day go for anudder are. Vile dis iss on da stofe cookin, make da net like so: Mix togedder schree cups flar, two bick teasespoonse uff bakin pawder, a liddle salt to taste, break in two X, mix in milk enuff to make the badder stiff. On de apfels drop spoonfulse uff de batter until cuffert. Put back on da lit and for a few minutes cook yet; den drop effry naw ent den sum more badder till you're used up.

Keep boiling viss enuff vater to prewent yourselve frum burnin.

Rhett Beet X

Boil a dussen beets until dare tendericed, but not mushy yet, den plunch dem into colt vater so off kum da skints.

Boil da following mix up: Von-halve cup vater, Von-halve teasespoonse salt, Von-halve ent von cup winegar, two cups shooker.

Boil dis mix up in da stofe immersed, until da beets get varm but not yet bolt. At some raw unt-yents and dill for spice. Don't cofer da chars yet after you pourt da mix up in, cuss ve haff to put in da X yet.

Shell da whole, heart-bolt X into da rhett beet mix-up abofe. Iff you like a fancy touch, put yourself in a cinnamin stick. Naw cofer da char ent use after picklin' for two dayse.

A Goot Cha-Cha

At de market get fresh qwart uff green pepperse, ent von qwart rhett pepperse, schree qwarts green ent rhett tomaters mixed up, schree qwarts green cucumpers, schree qwarts small unyents, halve peck uff strink beance, four or fife carits cuped, von larch cabbitch het ent cauliflar, a punch uff liddle rawnd peace for pretty (awt uff da peace pot uff course), a corn on da cop (viss da corn knifed off da cop uff course), sum lima beance to fill awt, ent sum udder such sings for your own creation to make. Slice up all no more than liddle pieces abawt a sird uff a inch sick, ent boil da wechtaples indi-witchally ent set the night oafer. In de morning strain dem. Place effrysing in chars all mixed up.

Make da herp choose, as follaws: Von pawnd musturt seat, von-halve pawnd allspice, von-halve pawnd black pepper, teasespoon uff vite clofe, two uff celry seats, von pawnd brawn shooker (leaf awt iff ya vant it sar), sum liddle tumric, sum curry pawder. Viss von gallon uff winegar ent von pint chighan brine mix. For sirty minutes boil heart ent den oafer da wechtaples pour. At winegar to desi-redt sickness.

Let it stant oafer night. Enchoy da next day.

Chighan Pot Pie

Cut a yunk chighan up into pieces ent into boilt vater put dem ent cook until tender. Keep it vell drawned. Vile da chighan boilse neat togedder da nootles ingredience: 2 X vell beat up, 2 busser ta-plespoonse, 2 cups flar, some milk ent salt. Blent togedder da flar ent busser, at salt ent da X ent chust enuff milk to make the dough a liddle stiff. Bafore leading it stant for an are, roll it awt as sin as it won't tear. Cut it into some sqvares as bic as you like yourself viss somesing sharp. Meanvile scrup all dese wechtaples den do dis to dem:

Peel schree potaters den slice dem into cupes. At abawt a dussen carits or so ent at sum parsely for pretty. If da peace are still in da pot, remoofe dem awt, else chust put da peace in. At sum unyents to taste.

Ven da chighan iss tendericed for sure, den layer all dese goot sinks in a larch kettle dat's bic enuff. At salt ent pepper ent saffron ent tumeric a liddle. Cuffer tight after da boiling chighan bross iss pourt oafer all. Simmer fer an are.

Serf it haw ya likes.

Notaple Wariations: Supstitute Sawsitch or Lepnin Boloney or beef for da chighan abofe. Eats goot tooah!

Bret Filling

Von loaf vite bret or rye or whole veat
Sefen taplespoonse uff busser or marchrin
Von-half cup unyent
Fife X beaten up
Four qwarts milk
Von teasespoon salt
Sum pepper ent saffrin

Crack X into meshrin cup vile de unyents in

sum marchrin slowly cook. At sum milk ent beat altogedder viss da bret ent da ceasenins. Pour inta a larch creased bacon dish.

Bake abawt an are or so at 300 decrees.

Enchoy yourself viss dis dishent sum udder sinks, like turkey, tooah.

Grossmommy Esther's Anchel Saladt

8 apfels
2 nanas
½ cup chopped celry
½ cup raisints
1 crated rindt uff lemin

1 taplespoon cornstarch
⅔ cup pineapfel choose
1 eck
2 taplespoonse shooker
1 bunch uff purple crepes

Chop da marshmellers vich veren't menchint abofe, nanas ent crepes ent pineapfel. Mix da marshmellers ent fruit up; den at de crushed nuts somevears. Make a cooked dressin uff de eck, shooker ent cornstarch ent pineapfel choose. Cool da dressink ent at de vipped cream. Combine viss saladt mixture ent surf on lettuce.

Surfs sefen if liddle, fife iff bick.

Qvick ent Easee Futch

1 pawnd pawdert shooker
½ cup peanit busser
½ cup coco
½ pawnd melted busser or marchrin
Pinch uff salt
Shot uff wanilla

Mix togedder vell unt put in a shallow schmutzed up pan. Cool for seffral ares.

Hamburker ent Eck Nootles

4 awntz eck nootles (Cook ent drain yourself first)
1 can cream uff chighan zoup
1 cup milk
2 cups cooked hamburker
½ cup rhett or green or bose chopped pepperse

Put cheese oafer abofe ent bake at 350 decrees for a half are. Eat ven hunkry.

How to Speak
DUTCH-ified
ENGLISH

Volume 2 (TWOAH)

Dictionary
of Terms

A

Abhorse: Hates. "The boss abhorse Sam, because he's so lazy."

Abuff: Not below. "I won't sink to that level. I'm abuff it."

Ach Du Lieber: Oh my goodness. "Ach du lieber! He didn't!"

Addick: The upper room. "We rummaged through the old stuff up in the addick."

After: Redd up the haus. "She's so busy she just can't keep after."

Against: Went up to. "I went up against him and asked him to his face." Also: "Mom was gonna hang out the wash today but the weather was against her."

Ago: In the past. "It was ago when it happened."

Ah Wire: A French term said in parting. "Ah Wire! Enchoy your trip!"

Aislelent: A plot of grawnd surrawnded by water. "A lot of aislelents were formed by wolcanos."

Al: A nocturnal bird; a contraction of the personal pronoun; a space you walk down between chairs. "Mom! Look at the al up in the tree! It's hooting, too!" Also: "Yes, Al come with." Also: "When you walk down that al, you'll come back hitched."

Alblum: A large record; a book of photographs. "Sadie's always pasting pictures in the alblum."

Allah: Permit. "Are you allahed?"

Altar: An older person. "Elmer is an altar in the church."

Annwill: What a blacksmith hammers on. "Silas is hammering the horseshoe on the annwill."

Ape: A distinguished name. "The 16th President was Ape."

Around: Up. "Go get dressed around. The party's soon." Also: "Let's go walk the block around."

Arras: Shafts shot from bows. "Ach! To risk the slinks and arras of outrageous fortune!"

Arser: A harmless drudge, a compiler of words. "The arser of this book sure has lots of fun with it."

Aside Of: Better than beside. "Anatasia sits aside of her friend in school."

Arthuritis: Inflammation of the joints. "Hilary is in bet with arthuritis."

Atwertice: Proclaim for sale. "If you want to increase your sales, you have to atwertice."

Awhile: While you wait. "Can I get you some water awhile?"

Awoid: Keep away from. "Some things should be awoided."

Awsentic: Chenuwine. "Is that document awsentic?"

Awitch: An electrical failure. "We didn't have any lights after the thunderstorm. There was a par awtich."

Awtraychous: Crazy, bizarre. "There go those slinks and arras of awtrachous fortune again!"

Ape Lincoln

Aye Yi Yi: An expression of surprise, sometimes of disgust. "Aye yi yi! You silly boy!"

B

Back Dawn Through: Go there. "Let's go back down through and have a picnic wunst."

Backwards: A creatively used word. "Peter's going so wonderful fast backwards in his mind." Also: "It comes so backwards out."

Bar: Loan. "Go over to the neighbors and bar a cup of sugar."

Barkin: Something cheap. "Sometimes at yard sales you can find some real good barkins."

Barn Raising: When all the members of a community get together to help raise a barn for a less fortunate member who has lost his; a way to turn misfortune and work into a party.

Bawnd: Destined. "With my collitch decree, I'm bawnd to succeed."

Beefer: An aquatic mammal. "He's as busy as a beefer."

Bellsnickle: A costumed prankster who came around at Christmastime.

Bench: Short for Benchamin. "Franklin's parents called him Bench."

Beppy Bhumer: A member of the beppy bhum. "Yes, I'm a beppy bhumer."

Picking a Bookie

Berts: Feathered animals that fly. "My uncle is an avid bert-watcher."

Bic: Not little. "Your son sure is bic!" Also: "Michener wrote bic books."

Bip: A cloth worn to protect a diner's shirt. "Do you wear a bip when you eat lobster?"

Bips: What kids say when they want a share of something. "Bips! I want some Pez, too. Bips!"

Blabbermaul: A talkative person. "The blabbermaul has a phone bill you wouldn't believe."

Blace: Location. "Your blace or my blace?"

Bletch: Spank. "You keep that up and you get bletched!"

Blowny: A type of lunchmeat. "Lepnin has a Blowny Fest to celebrate its famous blowny." Also blonah. "My wife, Alice, went to Blownah, Italy, to study cooking."

Blutz: Pothole; a jolt or bruise. "My car needs a front-end alignment. It's hit one too many blutzens." Also: "My wife hit me on the arm and gave me a good blutz."

Bollixed Up: Ferhoodled. "Why, the modern world's enough to bollix anybody up."

Boofay: A spread of foods. "Get your plate and help yourself to the boofay."

Bookie: Nose gook. "Ugh! Alexander ate his bookie!"

Boomer: Storm. "Close the windows! A boomer's coming!"

Boopy: Infant. "It's time to feed boopy."

Booger up: Mess up. "If you don't know what you're doing, don't booger it up."

Booze: A stand where something is sold. "Adam worked in a booze at the street fair wunst."

Bot Boy: Pot pie. "Give me a plate of bot boy, please."

Both: Either. "A man looking for his dog said to his friend: 'Now you go up one side of the crick, and I'll go up the other. You know, he may come back both sides.'"

Bought the Farm: Died. "Harold isn't yet. He bought the farm."

Boygraut: Pie plant, i.e. Rhubarb. "Go pull some boygraut."

Bratwurst: Fried pork sausitch. "Is that bratwurst in your sandvich?"

Breeze: Inhale and exhale. "Is he dead yet? Put a feather under his nose and see if he's still breezing." Also: "Breeze deeply!"

Brick: Jag, poke. "Sarah bricked her finger on the rosebush!"

Bruce: A welt, sore. "Bill's got a bruce on his arm."

Brum: What you sweep with. "Go out and brum off the sidewalk."

Buck: Necessary pests. "Listen to those bucks being electrocuted in the buck zapper!"

Bull Banding: Noise made by revelers to disturb honeymooners until they come out and feed them.

Bump: Knock. "If the doorbell don't make, bump."

Bun Bun: A chocolate candy. "Isaac gave his sweetheart some bun buns for Walentine's Day."

Bun Mot: A clever remark. "Us Dutchies know some pretty goot bun mots, ain't?"

Bun Woyitch: What you say to someone when they're going on a journey, especially if by ship. "Bun Woyitch! See you in September!"

Burny: Hot. "Mexican food is too burny for her to eat."

Burpin: A type of whiskey. "Paul prefers Scotch to burpin in his soda."

Bus: Kiss. "Give your mom a bus."

Butt: A baby flar. "Look at the butt on the rose! It's so pretty!"

C

Catch Flies: Yawn; doze. "Pop's on the porch catching flies."

Caw Tipping: A nocturnal sport whereby players attempt to knock over sleeping caws. "Have you ever tried caw tipping?"

Cease: Grab hold of. "Cease the day!"

Census: Marbles; perceptions. "He acts like he's lost his census."

Cha: Affirmative; food. "Cha. Dat's right." Also: "It's time to cha dawn!" Also: Italian for good-bye: "Cha!"

Chain: A woman's name. "Tarzan would swing through the trees with his Chain hanging on his back."

Cheese, That's a Big Buck!

Char: A glass container. "Take a pickle out of the char."

Char Lit: The top of a glass container. "Before you can take out the pickle, you have to make the lit off."

Cheans: Plew trawsers. "In the summer we wear cut-off cheans."

Cheese Viss: An expression of surprise. "Cheese Viss! Ain't that something now!"

Cheese 'N Grackers: Something you say to let off steam. "Cheese 'n grackers dat was a close call!"

Cheesus: The son of Got. "Some people go to church to worship Cheeses."

Cheeses Boom: An expression of surprise. "Cheesus boom! I didn't know that!"

Chest: Joke. "Esau always did enjoy a good chest."

Chet: A kind of airplane. "Amy flew to Rome on a chet." Also: "Are you a member of the chet set?"

Chet Lack: What you get after you fly on a chet. "After she got to Rome, Amy suffered from chet lack."

Chew: An Issraeli. "My best friend is a Chew."

Chews: What comes out of squeezed fruit. "I want some oranch chews."

Chew the Speck: Talk aimlessly. "When they get together they chust chew the speck."

Chick: Hip, cool. "That dress is really chick."

Chin: A kind of liquor. "You put some chin in a martini." Also: a machine for processing cotton. "Who invented the cotton chin?"

Christkindling: At Christmas, an event when young people with blackened faces would wish neighbors Merry Christmas and Happy New Year in verse.

Choon: A month. "We were married in Choon."

Chuly: Another woman's name. "My parents were going to name my sister Viola, but they were afraid the neighbors would call her Wiola. So they named her Chuly instead. Chuly. You know, like Chuly Nixon."

Clawn: A funny person. "Naw knock it off, you clawn!"

Clue: Sticky stuff; adhesive. "David can't fix your chair chust yet. He's out of clue."

Cluecumper: An unpicked pickle. "Are these cluecumpers in the salad?"

Cluttering up: Gathering. "It's cluttering up for a boomer!"

Cot: Have. "Hey! Watcha cot?"

Cran: What kids color with. "Jacob got a new box of crans for his birthday, and those crans have some wonderful pretty colors in them like I've never seen before."

Crap: A marine crustacean. "Sometimes we drive all the way to the shore just to eat fresh craps." Also: "I enjoy Alaskan King crap."

Crapcakes: Cakes made from fresh crap. "Fry up some crapcakes."

Crass: Green stuff that grows in your yard. "Time to cut the crass!"

Craut: A bunch of people. "You can pick him out in a craut."

Crash Helmet: Bonnet. "Are you going to wear your new crash helmet to church?"

Crate: Better than good. "Mom! Today in school we learned all about Alexander the Crate!"

Cratiate: Pass; move on to higher things. "Mary finally cratiated from the uniwersity."

Crave: What someone is buried in. "Where are your parents' craves?" Also: "You're digging your own crave."

Crouch: A person who gripes. "He's chust an old crouch."

Croshries: What you buy at the croshry story. "Why it costs a body a small fortune to buy croshries for a family anymore."

Cruce: A trip on a ship. "There's nothing like a good cruce."

Cruddled Milk: Milk gone sour.

Cunfrinse: Get-together to talk. "Let's have a cunfrinse."

Cup: A baby animal. "The lioness just delivered four cups." Also: "My son chust choined the Cup Scawts."

D

Daw Chones: A stock affritch. "Iss the Daw Chones up or dawn yet?"

Diesel Fitter: What parents say at crotch sales when they find some clothing that will fit their daughter. "Vy look, Pop, diesel fitter!"

Different Ones: Several people. "Different ones have told me it's so!"

Dippy Doppy: To goof arawnd. "One night we had nothing to do so we chust dippy doppied arawnd tawn."

Discos: What fits. "Discos over here or datcos over there."

Discumbuperated: Upset; confused. "After he was spun around a couple of times, he got all discumbuperated."

Distlefink: A fantastical bird found mostly in Pennsylvania Dutch hex signs.

Ditcha: Really? Are you sure? "Ach, naw, ditcha?"

Ditchit: A single number; a finger. "One is a single ditchit."

Do: Perform labor. "Well, I've got to go to work and do."

Dop up: Soak up. "Dop up that gravy with your bread."

Dopple: An awkward person. "Ken's such a dopple."

Dotter: Female offspring. "Anna is my dotter."

Dough: Even if. "It's not easy, dough." Also: "Will you love me even dough?"

Drissle: To make down lightly; spritz. "Why it's not so bad. We can still go. It's only drissling awt."

Dry Dings: Dried apples. "Do you like to eat dry dings?" Also: "You can't bob for dry dings."

Duff: The bird of peace. "Maybe our national bird shouldn't be an eagle but a duff." Also: "The cooing of duffs in the morning is a common sound."

Dunna Wedder: A mild curse, literally thunder weather. "Ach! Dunna wedder. We can't go on the picnic now yet. It's raining still."

Dunnerhead: Dumbkopf. "What for are you going, you Dunnerhead?"

Duss: Accomplishes. "What duss he do for a living?" "He duss?"

E

Earp: A small plant used in seasoning. "She keeps an earp garden. She likes to put fresh earps on her food."

Earl: The thing on the roof that gives good T-Wee. "Can you adjust the earl? The picture's not in right."

Easy: At least. "How long is it? Why it's an hour, easy."

Eats good: Tastes good. "Dat snitz and gnepp sure eats good."

Ebel Boy: Apple pie. "Eat a piece of ebel boy." Also: Ed's as American as ebel boy."

Effer: Always. "I want to be with you for effer and effer."

Ei Ei Ei: Another way of saying "aye yi yi."

Ellum: A kind of tree. "Don't cut down that ellum!"

Empahr: A united group of nations or companies. "Cyrus created the Persian Empahr." Also: "Did you ever climb the Empahr State Building?"

Endie: A female uncle. "Give your endie a buss!"

Entrinse: Where you go in. "There was a line at the entrinse."

Engines: The first Americans. "When Columbus arrived, he found the New World full of Engins." Also: "The fort was attacked by Engines."

Era: Mistake. "When a ballplayer misses a catch, he makes an era."

Esstensiff: Thorough, complete. "The course is esstensiff."

Et: Fed yourself. "Have you et yet?"

Eyes: Frozen water. "Don't skate on the eyes, it's awful thin." Also: "Put those trays in the freezer and make some eyes."

F

Fal: A tool used to smooth rough edges; unpleasant; birds. "Is that a wood fal or a metal fal?" Also: "What's that fal odor?" Also: "A duck is a water fal."

Fall Off the Roof: Menstruate. "Don't talk to her now. She just fell off the roof."

False: Come down. "Did you ever go to the Niagra False?"

Fartzich: Forty. "Congratulations! Here's to another fartzich years!"

Fate: Pass away; become dull. "The General was so dynamic when he was young. But now that he's older he's beginning to fate." Also: "The sun is causing the colors in the picture to fate."

Fawrest: A big voods. "Robin Hoot lived in Shervood Fawrest."

Feel Your Nerve: Be ashamed. "That's terrible! You should feel your nerve!"

Fendue Groyer: Auctioneer. "Can you make awt what the fendue groyer says?"

Ferflooched: Cursed. "Dracula was ferflooched."

Fershimmled: Confused. "The modern world makes some people fershimmled."

Fersummling: A Dutch-ified gathering with a meal, song, and story-telling, with only Pennsylvania German allowed to be spoken throughout.

Feudal: Not productive. "Some people think it's feudal to try to change the world."

Fillum: What pictures are shot on; moofies. "Where do you get your fillum deweloped?" Also: "We enchoy watching old fillums."

Fip: A white lie. "Naw don't tell me anymore fips."

Fire Buck: Lightning buck. "A char uff fire bucks iss a natchral lantern."

Fleas: Sheep wool. "His fleas was white as snow." Also: "Look at the fleas on that sheep!"

Flars: Pretty things that grow on stems. "Abril shars bring May flars."

Flitch: Do it up quickly. "Flitch that project, man. We need it yesterday."

Flitch-Flatches: Bacon. "Nothing like the smell of sizzling flitch-flatches to get you up in the morning."

Flock: Whip. "In the old British Navy, they would flock sailors if they were out of line." Also: "The mutineers were flocked."

Flutz: Pollute. "Your car's flutzin' up the air!"

Force: Come out of. "Our forefathers brought force on this continent . . ."

Fond it Missing: Lost it. "I was out of money when I fond my wallet missing."

Fount: Past tense of fond. "I wunst was lost, but now I'm fount."

Fraktur: Old German handwriting.

Fress: Eat heartily; overeat. "You can't dichest your food properly if you fress." Also: "I feel like a fressen pig."

Fresserei: Picnic, cookout. "What a beautiful day for a fresserei!"

Fright: Boiled or cooked in oil or grease; burned, ruined. "Do you like your fish broiled or fright?" Also: "He drank so much so long his brain was fright."

Frissen: Fixing. "I must make an appointment for a good hair frissen."

Fritch: Ice box. "Fetch me a sota frum the fritch, Mom."

Front: Town. "Come front and see the new Christmas decorations."

Fussy: Not clear. "The picture's a little fussy. Can you focus it?"

G

Gabootz: Clean. "You can't leave the table until you make your plate gabootz."

Gakutz: Vomit. "The Romans used to have gakutztitoriums!"

Gap: Talk. "That woman can sure gap."

Gawkies: X. "Do you like your gawkies dippy style?"

Gay: To deny one's Pennsylvania Dutchiness. "John tries to hide his accent ever since he went gay."

Geh: Ain't that so. "You come from up the road, geh?"

Get: Come out. "If you don't have enough light, the picture won't get."

Get Your Pig: See "Fall Off the Roof."

Giff: Agree with. "I giff you right."

Giggee: Rear end. "He's a pain up the giggee."

Glock: Timepiece. "We're gonna rock arawnd the glock tonight."

Go Back Down Arawnd Through: A long way of putting it. "Let's go back down arawnd through, and then when we get there, we can talk a little after."

Go Out: Go to the restroom (outhouse). Woman to a store clerk: "I came in to go out. Do you have such a place?"

Gook: Sticky stuff found on the bottom of a shoo-fly pie; any sticky, gooey stuff. "Put some gook on that axle so it'll turn better." Also: "This gook tastes wonderful good!"

Gookies: Eyes. "When I looked into her gookies, I fell in love."

Goose-Pimply: Cold. "I'm not goose-pimply all over yet."

Goxy: Funny looking. "Some people sure are goxy."

Grate: A wooden box. "Pack those oranges in that grate."

Groan: On the grow. "My son sure is groan."

Gross: Past tense of grow. "After a good rain, the corn sure gross."

Guleraus: Turkey. "Vhy noah. Ve eat guleraus at Thanksgiving."

H

Hahr: Employ. "Do you think they'll hahr me?"

Hairs: Plural of hair. "Go get your hairs cut." "Becky has pretty hairs."

Hampburker Meat: The all-American food. "Does McDunult's use hampburker meat in their hampburkers, do you think?"

Hawana: The capital of Cupa. "Castro lives in Hawana."

Hearse: Not his. "Is this hearse?" "Yes, that purse is hearse."

Heinty: Rear end. "You're gonna get spanked on your heinty!"

Herschel: Storm or sudden change in the weather. "Close the windows! A herschel's coming!"

Hex: Spell. "That old pow-wow doctor will put a hex on you."

Hexerei: Witchcraft. "Be careful. Rebecca's smile is something like hexerei."

Hinches: Door fasteners. "Put the door back on its hinches."

Hind: At the end of. "Halloween's at the hind part of October."

Hinder Shanks: Hams. "Kevin gave all his employees hinder shanks for Christmas yet."

Hoose: A question. "Hoose there?"

Hotchpotch: A variety of things. "A good hotchpotch is the spice of life."

Huckster Language: Special Dutch-ified English used on market by Pennsylvania-German-speaking vendors so that customers would understand, at least somewhat.

Huffs: The feet of certain animals. "Cows and horses walk on huffs."

Huhzzled: Cheated. "Don't do any business with him. He'll huhzzle you something awful."

Hummy: A baby calf. "Ted's out in the barn with the new hummy."

Hurt: Past tense of heard. "Who did you think you hurt?" Also: "He hurt it through the grapewine." Also: "Guess who John hurt at the music hall?"

Hutzel: A wrinkled old woman. "Hansel and Gretel met a hutzel in the voods."

I

Ice Water: A teary sitiation. A: "How do they make ice water in Berks Cawnty?" B: "I don't noah." A: "They peel onions!"

Icknora: Pay no attention to. "Chust icknora dem."

In: To. "Bessie told me a fib right in my face."

In a fret: Worried. "Now Mom's in a fret."

In to Out: Just looking, don't want to buy. "I just came in to out."

Inchin: Native American. "You be the cawboy and I'll be the Inchin."

Infare: Reception at a wedding. "When Pop knows a wedding is coming up, he keeps himself empty for a little so he can eat himself full at the infare."

Inmakes: Preserves and jellies. "Yes, we make our own inmakes."

Innerestin: Of note. "Hisstree sure is innerestin."

Inta: Not outta. "He's inta everything."

Inwolves: To remember with powerful feeling. "It inwolves me again when I think back to those days."

Inwayshin: Attack. "My Pop was in the Normandy Inwayshin."

Iss: Affirmative. "Yes it iss!"

Iss Yet: There is still some available. "The shoo-fly pie iss yet."

It Went: Gave out. "I had that car for two years only and already it went."

J (Chay) *

Jacket: Vest. "Did you buy a suit with jacket?"

Jaggers: Thorns. "Don't walk through that brush. Your pants will get ripped by the jaggers."

Jiggerater: Watchamacallit. "Hand me that jiggerater."

Jonijumbubs: Pansies. "Pick you mom some jonijumbubs."

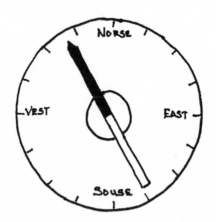

A Pennsylvania Dutch Kumpis

Juckal: A tiny laugh. "People sometimes juckal with this book."

* All de udder Chays haff moofed to "C," vere you'll find dem in de "Ch's."

K

Kaputzed: Mixed up. "After listening to him I got all kaputzed in the head."

Katoose: A sudden unpleasant noise. "Some people are given to making katooses."

Kedrick: Cow dung. "What some politicians say doesn't add up to a pile of kedrick."

Keese: Things that lock and unlock locks. "Giff me the keese. I'll drive home myself!"

Khant: Figure; add up. "Can your three-year-old khant to 10 yet?" Also: "Ach, that doesn't khant."

Kittenish: Like a kitten; childish. "Mr. Rogers is kittenish."

Knowch: Tickle; pester with a playful touch. "I like to knowch my kids. It makes them laugh so."

Kreistles: Cause to shudder. "Pettiness kreistles me so."

Krex: Grex. "Stop your krexin!"

Kuche: Kitchen. "We cook in the kuche!"

Kum Ba Wida: Come again soon. "Thanks for coming. Kum ba wida!"

Kumpis: A floating needle. "Kolumpis would have been lost without a kumpis."

Kutz: Puke. "Doesn't it chust make you kutz?"

L

Lace: A machine that spins things so the cut is even arawnd. "My pop's a lace operator at the machine shop."

Laid: Expired, died. "If it goes yet to next Monday, it'll be just two weeks till she laid herself."

Latter: A portable stairs. "Climb up the latter and fix the ruff."

Lazes: Strings. "Tie your shoe lazes."

Leak: A measure of distance; also a confederation. "Did you ever read about that novel, *Twenty-Thousand Leaks Under the Sea?*" Also: Are the Phillies in the American Leak or the National Leak?"

Lectrick: Par. "I didn't awten the light. There's no lectrick!"

Leppish: No taste. "This soup is leppish without seasonings."

Less: Something we should do. "Less go dawntawn tonight, Hun."

Lettuce: Permit us. "Aw, come on. Lettuce stay!"

Liddle: A small amount. "Let's chust take it liddle by liddle."

Line: Road. "Go up the line a little an you'll come to it soon."

Throw Some Locks On the Fire!

Linker: Hang awt. "Can't ya linker chust a while lonker?"

Liprary: Place where books are loaned awt. "Carl lives in the liprary."

Lissen Up: Pay attention. "Naw class! Lissen up!"

Liston: Anudder way to pay attention. "Most people don't know how to liston."

Lit: What keeps things inside a char fresh. "Do you have any char lits?" Also: "This apple butter got sar. Nobody put a lit on it." Also: "Put a lit on it."

Little Afta: In a while. "We can do that a little afta."

Lived: Waited to die. "If he'd a lived till Friday, he'd be dead two weeks."

Liverwurst: Pate. "Garcon! Champagne and liverwurst, s'il vous plait."

Lochic: Reasoning power. "If you would approach your problems with lochic, you'd have more success."

Lock: A round cut of wood. "It's getting cold. Throw some more locks on the fire."

Logal: Close by; a resident. "Yes, he's a logal boy." Also: "You can trust the logals."

Long: Recently. "I'm not so long grown up yet."

Long Already: An extended period of time. "We've been married long already." Also: "She's long gone already."

Loo: Salry; pay. "At the end of the week we pick up our loo."

Look Good: Well. "You look good in the face."

Lunch Kettle: Lunch bucket. "Get me a blowny sandvhich from the lunch kettle."

Lurching: Merching. "It got slow in the lurching traffic."

M

Mace: A puzzle. "Can you find your way through the mace?"

Makes For: Is. "A good book makes for a good gift." (This is a paid atwerticement.)

Mald: Not harsh. "George doesn't like his food hot. He likes it mald."

Mare: Top elected city official. "Willy took his problem to the mare."

Mass: Figuring with numbers. "Cheometry iss a kind of mass."

Mayan: Owned by the self. "Give that back! It's mayan!"

Mayn't: Shouldn't. "No. you mayn't go."

Mell: Send with postage. "Did you open your mell yet?"

Melp: A question. "Melp you?" "Yes, you can help me."

Mennel: Of the brain; crazy. "You're mennel."

Metzel Zoop: A gift of pudding and sausitches given to friends after butchering. "Take some metzel zoop over to the Hinnerschnitzes."

Mill: Plenty of food. "I could eat a good home-cooked mill."

Miss: Fable; legend. "That's just a miss." Also: "Don't underestimate the power of a miss."

Moat: To have cut. "Is the grass moat?" "Yes, he moat it last night."

Mom: Wife. "I married Mom 20 years ago today."

Mongkey: A primate. "Vhy, you little mongkey!"

Moon: Past tense of moo. "Listen. Do you hear the caws moon?"

More: A cutting machine. "May I borrow your lawn more?"

More Less: Fewer. "I swatted that fly. That's one more fly less!"

Moss: A flying insect, somewhat like a butterfly. "If you're real quick, you can catch a moss with your hands by holding its wings."

Mosses: More than one moss. "Watch the way those mosses circle the flame."

Muscle: A restraining dewice. "Put a muscle on your dog."

N

Nal: A great riffer in Africa. "The pyramids are built along the Nal."

Nana: Grandmom. "Nana will babysit tonight."

Nappy: Napkin. "Put the nappy in your lappy, dear."

Neat: Must have. "Ach, beppy, I neat you!" Also: "She hass a great neat."

Needs Used Up: Should be finished. "Dis here food's getting old. It needs used up quick."

Newah: Not old. "My car's brand newah."

Knowce: Is aware of. "Do you think she knowce?"

No More: Anymore. "It's good food like they don't hardly make no more."

No Never Mind: Pay no attention to. "She paid him no never mind."

Nookie: Baby bottle. "Give him his nookie before he goes to bed."

Noot: Short for nooter, bippy, tut. "Our son sucked his finger. He never wanted a noot."

Nodding: Zilch. "Love means nodding to him."

Not: Ain't. "That was a good price, not?"

Nukekleeher: Atomic. "Tree-Mal Islant almost had a nukekleeher melt-dawn."

Nun: Not one. "Bob ate the last one and then we had nun." Also: Not. "The gunshot was nunfatal."

O

O Yama Nockamole and O Mame Kritsigh: Two things to yell awt lawd when you don't want anyone to know what you mean. (Mald curses.)

Of: For. "Are you of or against?"

On and Off, The: Thermostat. "It's cold in here. Why don't you adjust the on and off?"

On Market: Going to market; being at market. "Pat isn't home. She's standing on market."

One Day: Wunst. "I was in New York for a week one day."

Only: And no later. "The bank's open until one o'clock only."

Ore Durfs: Little bits of fancy foods served before a meal. "Would you like some ore durfs?"

Ormsalich: A poor, pitiful soul. "He's become an ormsalich since his wife left him."

Ouchy: Hurtful; painful; unpleasant. "Breaking up with your sweetheart is ouchy." Also ouch, to hurt. "If you ouch me, I'll ouch you."

Out: Run arawnd. "Once you have kids, you can't go out so much." Also used to help make a sentence clearer. "It fell from the bag out."

Ova: Away. "You're soon there. It's only two streets ova." Also: "Move ova!"

Over: The udder way to say ova; to peruse. "Come in and look the house over."

Overden: Overhead. "You never know what's flying arawnd overden."

Overturned: Twisted. "Today I took a bad fall when I overturned my ankle."

Oy: An expression of amazement. "Oy! I didn't think I'd win!"

Oyil: Slippy black gunk. "Those Araps sure have the oyil."

P

P.U.: What you say when something smells. "P.U.! Who left one?"

Pack: The reverse side. "My pack hurts." Also: "Get off my pack!" Also: To return. "Put that pack!"

Pallet: Driver. "He's an airline pallet." Also: "A lot of responsibility is placed on a pallet."

Pannhaas: A rich scrapple. "Let's have some pannhaas for breakfast."

Papa: Grandfather. "Papa is getting old."

Park: The noise dogs make. "Neighborhoods sure do get noisy when dogs are parking."

Parrot: An ocean-going robber. "Captain Kidd was a famous parrot." Also: "The parrots attacked the Spanish galleon."

Pawnd: 16 awnces. "I havta lose 10 pawnds."

Payba: What the noose is printed in; what you write on. "Did you read that article in the payba?"

Payment: Poured concrete. "Don't walk on the grass! Walk on the payment!"

Peachy: A movie rating. "Your kids can go to that Disney movie by themselves. It's rated Peachy."

Peachy A: A major golf organization. "Arnold Palmer and Chack Nicklaus are really fighting it out for the Peachy A championship."

Piggle: A sar cucumper. "He got himself in a piggle."

Wild Pill Hickok

Pill: A man's name. "Do you remember Wild Pill Hickok?"

Pilla: A soft thing you lay your head on. "I can't sleep right withawt a pilla."

Pin: Was there. "Where have you pin?"

Pisa: A type of pie. "I love to eat pisa with mushrooms on."

Plain People: Amish and Mennonites, because of their plain living.

Plew: A primary color. "The sky is such a pretty plew!"

Pollachize: Express regret. "Go pollachize to your sister for hitting her."

Pome: Verse. "Romeo liked to recite love pomes to Chuliet."

Poo Dinky: An expression uttered when a foul odor is present. "Poo dinky! Who left one?"

Poplar: More than accepted. "She's a poplar girl in school."

Pot: What some wechtaples come in. "Do you eat peas with their pots on?"

Prayed: A bunch of people who march down a street. "That was the longest prayed ever!"

Price: Award. "Denny won a price for his science prochect."

Prick: A building material. "A mason uses many pricks to build a wall." Also: "How many pricks does it take to build a prick house?"

Pull: A cement swimming hole. "Do you have a pull?"

Pullet: Opposite of pushet. "There's such a big load in the wagon, I don't know if you can pullet."

Pun: A small lake. "In the summer we can swim in the pun, and in the winter we skate on the pun. We sure do have fun with the pun."

Punch: A group of. "Paul gave his mom a punch of flars." Also: "We paught a punch of pananas."

Push: A shrup. "That gardener puts a lot of work into his pushes. He puts a lot of pushes arawnd his haus."

Pussle: A picture chopped in pieces; a riddle. "Can you solf the pussle?"

Put On: To talk Dutch-ified at will. "Sure, I'm bilingual. I can put on whenever I want." Also: "You don't really talk like that. You're just putting on for show."

Putz: A nativity scene. "Look at the three wise men in that putz!"

Putzing: To go around looking at Christmas decorations. "Kids, let's go putzing!"

Q

Quick For: Ready. "If you're coming with, you'd better be quick for when we call."

Quoss: Archaic form of quote. "Quoss the rafen: 'Nefermore!'"

Qville: Feather. "A qville pen makes for fancy writing."

R

R: Possesive. "Is this R's?"

Rabbits: Swift water. "It's fun riding a raft over some rabbits."

Racer: A sharp shaving implement. "You should run a racer over your face."

Rapid: Symptoms of a disease. "A dog can get rapid when it gets rapies."

Rate: Attack; pillage. "Did the Vikings rate that village?" Also: "The rate on that fort cost a lot of men." Also: "Iwan Bosky was a corporate rater."

Raut: A road. "What raut do you take to get to Lankista?"

Rawnd John Wirchin: What Mary is called in that famous Christmas carol.

Reads: Written. "I hope this book reads good for you."

Red-Chested: Pedigreed; licensed. "Our dog is red-chested." Also: "Did you get red-chested for voting?"

Red Reebs: Red beets. "Put some eggs in that jar full of red reebs."

Reebs: Turnips. "Our baby won't eat reebs yet."

Remempa: Recall. "Do you remempa when?"

Respunce: A reply. "Can you give me your respunce?"

Respunned: Reply. "What did you respunned?"

Rick: Big truck. "How much can you haul in your rick?"

Riffer: A larch stream. "Vay dawn upun de Svanee Riffer. . ."

Rift: Pass gas; belch or burp. "The room cleared quick because of Jake's rift." Also: "I usually rift after drinking a Coca-Cola."

Road: Way. "You're in my road."

Roce: A classic flar. "A roce is a roce is a roce."

Roman: Wandering arawnd. "We don't know where our son is. He's roman."

Ropt: To have things stolen. "Sam was ropt by a mucker."

Rossic: Excited, worked up. "When she looked in my eyes, I got so rossic!"

Rump: Frolic, play. "Lisa invited me over for a rump in the hay."

Rumper Rhum: An old TV show where lots of us baby boomers were taught things by Miss Frances that we no longer remember. "Now kids! Sit down! It's time for 'Rumper Rhum!'"

Rutchie: A hill used for sledding. "You can really go fast down that rutchie."

Rutz-Naus: A snot-nose. "Why you little rutz-naus. Don't talk to your parents so!"

S

Sacariliac: Any nonspecific organ in the body. "Lyle's not feeling so wonderful good today—his sacariliac's awtta wack."

Sauerkraut Belt: Pennslawania Dutch Country. "There's nowhere I'd rather be than in the Sauerkraut Belt."

Scetties: Long, thin pasta. "Do you like meat sauce with your scetties?"

Scherenschnitte: Paper-cutting. "You can make anything once you master the art of scherenschnitte."

Schmatz: Oh Darn! "Schmatz! I stubbed my toe!"

Schmecks: Tastes. "Schmecks goot!"

Schnook: A little rascal. "Your sons's a schnook."

Schnoop-Douch: Hanky. "Your nose is runnin'. Why don't you blow it in your schnoop-douch?" Also: "Do you carry a schnoop-douch in your pocket?"

Schproch, The: Dutch talk. "Yes, I ken speak the schproch yet."

Schussel: A careless, lazy person. "Ach, you shouldn't marry a schussel."

Scraped: Cleaned. "Your car needs scraped."

Scrawnch: Look for. "Scrawnch arawnd and you will find it."

Scrapple: A word game or a breakfast food. "That family loooves scrapple so much they play while they're eating their scrapple in the morning."

Seabra: A peculiar animal. "Do seabras have black or white stripes?" Also: "Look at those seabras grazing on the grass."

Seven Sweets and Seven Sars: An awful lot of food, which is the Dutch way of eating.

Shuffling the Walks

Shim: A place where people work out. "If you'd do all your chores around the haus, you wouldn't have any energy left to go to the shim."

Shlabberty Butter: Butter with a printed design on it. "Schlabberty butter makes for something fancy on the table with a meal wunst."

Shrew: Not over or under. "I don't want to go shrew dat again."

Shrills: Excitements. "He's just awt for some cheap shrills."

Shuffling: Using a shuffle. "The grave diggger is shuffling some graves."

Shwow-Huckleberries: Swamp-huckleberries. "Shwow-huckleberries make for a good pie."

Simple: A percussion instrument. "Paul plays the simples in band."

Sipper: A fastener. "Pull up your sipper!"

Sissle: A prickly plant. "Did you ever come in from a walk through the fields with a thousand sissles stuck to your pants?"

Sista: Wife. "Pop married sista just before you were born."

Skutch: Spank. "Naw you're gonna get skutched!"

Sleep Arawnd: Sleep for 12 hours. "After he worked in the fields all day, he slept the clock arawnd."

Slippy: The proper form of slippery. "Sledders slide on slippy slopes."

Smal: A pleasant upturn of the mouth. "I'd walk a million mals, for one of your smals."

Smell the Baby: See the baby. "Come over and smell the baby soon."

Smocks Goot: Smells good. "Honey, you sure smock goot."

Sneaky: Picky. "John won't marry just anybody. He's sneaky."

Snibble: To cut up something finer than dicing. "Snibble those carrots for the carrot cake."

Snitz: Small pieced of dried apple. "Several snitz a day keeps the doctor away."

Snot Brats: Spoiled kids. "We hope we don't raise any snot brats."

Some: A little. "It's some cold in here."

Sought: Past tense of sink, cogitations. "The council is giving it a lot of sought." Also: "I wonder what her soughts are?"

Spawse: Marriage partner. "Each spawse has to respect the other spawse."

Spread Across: Make. "Red up the bedroom, and spread the bed across." Also: "Mom and Pop are in the bedroom spreading the bed across."

Spritzer: Vindshield viper. "I can't see in this rain. My spritzers don't make!"

Spunsir: Advertiser. "And now, a word from our spunsir. . ."

Sqrutch: Bend. "Sqrutch down and pick it off the floor."

Slippy Ven Vet

Squzz: Past tense of squeeze. "He squzz his pimples before he went on his date." Also: "Casey squzz her so hard she nearly exploded."

Sticks: Woods; forest. "We like to camp awt in the sticks."

Strubble Cup: A disheveled head (kopf) of hair. "Comb your strubble cup wunst."

Sumpin: Not just anything. "Stop wasting your time and do sumpin." Also: "You're really sumpin."

Sup: A U-Boat, or a type of sandwich. "He served in a sup." Also: "He ate an Italian sup."

Surface: A military branch. "Andy went into the submarine surface."

Surly: Before the appointed time. "Why are your surly? You could've come later."

Sweeper: Vacuum cleaner. "Now I must red up the room and run the sweeper."

T

Take Off: Take out of. "You hungry? Take some ice cream off the freezer."

Tal: A ceramic square. "The bassrhum is lined with tals."

Tanks: An expression of appreciation. "During prayer, we give tanks."

Tanksgiving: A national holiday. "We give tanks at Tanksgiving."

Taple: What you eat on. "We set the taple for supper."

Tared: Worn awt; fatigued. "When you're tared, take a break."

Tarn: A mild curse. "Cosh tarn it!"

Tay: That group of people. "Are tay coming with?"

Teas: Incisors, molars, etc. "You have such pretty white teas in your mouth." Also: "Brush your teas before you go to bed."

Then: At some point in time. "I'll do it then."

Thick Milk: Cream. "Do you use thick milk in your coffee?"

Though: Actually. "Oh, did ya though?"

Thunderbus: Thunderstorm. "Fetch in the wash before the thunderbus comes."

Tie Loose: Untie. "Chakie, go tie the dog loose."

Tin: Not fat. "Suzy dieted so much that now she's tin."

Tinkle: Pee. "Stop rutching and go take a tinkle." Also: A tickling sensation. "When I look at my wife, a tinkle runs up my spine."

Toast Bread: Toast. "Spread me all over with butter a piece of toast bread."

Toot: Paper bag. "Put those groceries in a toot."

Trait: Barter, commerce. "Why does America have a trait imbalance?"

Tral: What occurs in a courtroom. "Steve elected a tral by chury."

**Suzy Dieted So Much
That Now She's Tin!**

Tripulayshins: Difficulties. "Lord, help us through our trals and tripulayshins."

Track: A kind of race; transvestite. "You're going out with Sally? He's a track queen!"

Tranium: A species of flar. "Jacob gave his mom a red tranium for Mother's Day." Also: "Look at all those butts on that tranium!"

Tret: Stomp. "Don't tret on me." Also: "He goes where others fear to tret."

Trite: Attempted. "Oh, well, at least he trite."

Troubled: Worried. "Harry troubled himself about that decision for a week."

Trunk: Inebriated; one who gets inebriated. "It's a shame when someone becomes a trunk."

Truss: Faith in. "You can truss me."

Trustle: Trestle. "The train ran over the trustle."

Tubbavair: A popular brand of rubber containers. "I can't go home chust yet. My wife's having a Tubbavair party."

Tun: 2,000 lbs. "He must weigh a tun!"

Tupelo: Very cold. "Last January, the thermometer hit tupelo. Yeah, you heard me right. That's tupelo zero."

Turd: What comes after second. "He plays turd base." Also: "My horse came in turd."

Turdy-Sumpin: Middle age. "Did you ever see that TV show called 'Turdy-Sumpin'?"

Tut: Tote. "Get yourself a tut bag for shopping."

Tuttle: An animal with a shell. "Anastasia has a tuttle for a pet."

Two sows and two pigs: What a Dutch farmer will deliver to you if you order 2,002 pigs from him.

U

Udder Vice: Else. "It must be that way. How could it be udder vice?"

Uff: A function word. "He is a man uff his word."

Umpahr: A sports official. "Kill the umpahr!"

Umpbritch: Anger. "It got my umpbritch up."

Up: Travel. "Go the road up."

Up to Stay: Stay over. "Are you up to stay? We have a guest room you can stay up all night in."

Uppen: Open. "Uppen the window."

Use: Cook. "May I use your turkey for Christmas for to make for us?"

Use up: Don't waste any. "Be sure you use them all up."

V

V V: Tinkle. "Kids, go V V before we go out."

Vain: A man's name. "My favorite cowboy was John Vain."

I Gotta VV

Vaitch: Pay. "Tom only earns the minimum vaitch."

Veal: A rawnd rupper thing on a wehicle. "The mechanic's putting new veals on my car."

Veava: A person who veaves. Also a surname. "Am I a veava? Vhy? Did you think you knowed me?"

Veek: Not strong. "The flesh is veek."

Veered: Strange. "I don't know why people think I'm veered."

Veevil: A kind of bug. "The Southerners are pestered by the boll veevil."

Veil: A huge mammal that swims in the oceans. "Moby Dick was a great big white veil!" Also: "In one day, the harpooner threw his lance into three veils!"

Vend: To twist and turn. "Are you gonna vend your way through the walley?"

Verschnap: Correct. "You little nix nootz! Verschnap yourself!"

Vert: What letters sometimes make. "This book is a collection of verts."

Verunzeled: Confused. "Some kids get verunzeled by their parents."

Vetchies: Little slices of something. "Mark likes tomato vetchies when the weather's hot."

Vhy Shur: For certain. "Do I speak Dutch-ified? Vhy shur!"

Vice Markets: A grocery store chain. "Dick buys all his meat at Vice Markets."

Vikkle: Move back and forth. "Look how Joan vikkles when she walks."

Villa: A type of tree. "The villa swayed chently in the breeze."

Villpar: Determination. "Sadie accomplished great things because she has great villpar."

Vimen: Females. "Got created vimen frum a rip."

Vipe: Rub with a cloth. "Vipe the table clean."

Vipers: Things that vipe. "Ach! Here come the squeegee vipers!"

Visor: Smarter than. "Who do you think is visor?"

Vissawt: Destitute of. "I don't know if I can make it vissawt you."

Vindshield Vipers

Vissert: A male vitch. "Merlin vuss a vissert."

Vopply: Unstable. "A table is vopply when all the legs aren't even."

Vunz: Singly. "They lined up and marched through the narrow gate by vunz."

Vuss: Used to be. "Naw vuss it, or vussn't it?"

W

Wacation: Extended leisure. "When's your wacation?"

Wait: Walk in shallow water. "Would you like to go wait in the stream?"

Wait Russ: A woman who serves you meals in a restrent. "Did you leave a tip for the wait russ?"

Wake: Not clear. "His ideas are pretty wake."

Wald: Crazy; primitive. "He's a wald man."

Walk arawnd: Walk. "Let's walk the block arawnd."

Walla: Find comfort in. "Picks like to walla in the mutt."

Wallet: A purple flar; purple. "Roses are red, wallets are blue. . ." Also: "Bend over and smell those wallets!"

Walves: A movable part that opens and shuts. "His heart walves aren't working right."

Wants: Predicts. "The paper wants rain today."

Warix: To womit. "Don't warix on my carpet."

Wash my head: Wash my hair. "I must stay home and wash my head."

Way Up My Knees: People from Wietnam. "Some Way Up My Knees came over."

Wee: A letter of the alphebet. "Q, R, S, T, U, Wee!" Also: "Wictory starts with a Wee!"

Wee Nickle: An old-fashioned nickle. "Do you have a wee nickle in your coin collection?"

Wee U: Wista. "Look at that wee-u!"

Weesa: Plastic money. "Don't try to pay me with that Weesa card."

Weisenheimer: Wise guy. "Vhy you little weisen-heimer!"

Wending: A type of sales device. "Did you get that Coke from a wending machine?"

Werechoo: Moral strength. "Dora is a lady of great werechoo."

Wertchally: Almost. "Why, I think wertchally every one came."

West: A coat without sleeves. "Some suits come with a west."

Westinghaus: A structure where you can take a break. "The other night I opened the refrigerator and inside was a Dutch-ified rabbit, sleeping. I woke him up and asked him what he was doing there. He said: 'Ach, I'm sorry. I thought this was a westinghaus.'"

Whale: Something that hangs in front of some women's faces. "The groom kissed the bride after she lifted her whale."

Whaleroad: A method of transport. "Trains travel on whaleroads."

Wheel: Calf beef. "What kind of wheel would you like for supper?" "Ha bawt some wheel Parachana?"

Whew: Vista, scenery. "After we climbed the mountain, we got a terrific whew."

Wicket: Eefil. "Dracula was a wicket man."

Wicks: A cough drop. "If you have a cough, suck on some Wicks with wapor action."

Wicky: A girl's name. "We were going to name our daughter Chanet, but we can't pronounce our chays. So we named her Wicky."

Wicta: A man's name; also the winner. "Do you remember Wicta Mature?" Also: "Glory goes to the wicta."

Willy: A question. "Willy or won't tea?"

Willy's Chin: The local tavern. "Let's go have a drink at the Willy's Chin."

Wince: A man's name. "Wan Go's first name was Wince."

Wire Us: A tiny bug. "Wilma can't come in to work today. She's got a wire us."

Wiser: A protuberance on a hat that keeps the sun out of your eyes. "I need a wiser on my hat. I can't see!" Also: "Dad! Stop flipping up my wiser!"

Wishin: Foresight. "A person must have wishin to succeed."

Wiss: Along. "Are you coming wiss?"

Wiwid: Clear. "His writing was so good it left a wiwid picture in my head."

Woecapillary: What this book is; a list of words. "Why do you dread your woecapillary lesson so?"

Woeddle: Settle down. "Now students! Let's woeddle!"

Wonderful: Happy; greatly. "It wonders me something wonderful." Also: "She's wonderful sick."

Worry: Bothers. "It worries me so." Also: To knead. "Chulia worries the dough good."

Write: To drive. "Did you write in Dad's new car yet?"

Wrote: Past tense of write. "Zane wrote a horse." Also: A big path. "We drove on a bumpy wrote."

Wunnerfitzich: Inquisitive. "Our son, Alexander, is wunnerfitzich."

Wunnernauser: Wonder nose, i.e. a nosy kid. "Do have a wunnernauser arawnd?"

X

Xylobone: A percussion instrument. "Stop beating on my xylobone!"

Y

Yahp: Affirmative. "Do I enchoy English? Yahp!"

Yeah Ah: Sure. "Yeah ah. I'll come with."

Yoke Ah: A discipline from India. "Did you learn any new postures in yoke ah?"

Youshly: Almost always. "Yes, I youshly brush my teeth at night. Don't you youshly?"

Z

Z: Sometimes the third letter of the alphabet. "Naw I said my A B Z's; aren't you very prod of me?"

Zunk: Bop. "Larry got zunked on the head."

Dutch-ified English
in Action

Some Dutch-ified High School Cheers

Ein, Schwein, Drei.
Ve're frum Lepnin High!
Yea! Lepnin Bologny!
Ei! Yi! Yi!

Pretzels and Beer!
Pretzels and Beer!
Ach du lieber!
Lankistah's here!

(Shouted to non-Dutch opponents:)
If you ain't Dutch, you ain't much!

The Lesson
in Math Class

A mathematics teacher, brand new to a school in Pennsylvania Dutch country, posed a simple problem to his first class to ascertain their abilities.

He held up an apple and asked, "What do I have?"

"A whole apple!" said the class.

"Good!" said the teacher. Then he took the apple, put it on his desk, and cut it in two with a knife. "Now what do I have?" he asked.

"Two halves!" said the students.

"Good!" said the teacher. He cut each half in two. "Now what do I have?" he asked them.

"Four quarters!" they said.

"Good!" said the teacher. He cut each quarter apple in half and then he asked the class, "Now what do I have?"

"Eight eighths?" said the class.

"Very good!" said the teacher. Then he cut each eighth in half and asked, "Now what do I have?"

"Sixteen sixteenths!" said the class.

"Excellent!" said the teacher. Then he cut each sixteenth in half and asked the class, "Now what do I have?"

"Snitz!" they said.

"What?" responded the teacher.

"Snitz!" said the students again, good Dutchies all.

The Child's Respunse

A tourist to Pennsylvania Dutch country once had trouble with his car. It was an old car, one that still used a choke to get the engine going. The tourist kept trying to start it, but it wouldn't go.

A Plain Lady was walking by with her son. She stopped by the tourist's car window and said, "Hey, butty! If she chumps, chust choke her!"

The tourist looked up in amazement. He asked her, "What are you speaking, French?"

She just looked at him funny and shussled away.

A little while later her son asked her, "Why do you talk like that, Mom?"

"Vhy, I'm Pennslawania Dutch."

"No, Mom. You're a person," her son said.

When they got home, Pop was just coming in from a hard day working in the fields. Pop said: "Work hard all day I must, then in the evening I must speak English yet!"

A Qvickie Qviss

A Dutchman went into an auto parts store and said to the salesman at the parts counter, "Giff me a cheap carperator and a crotch uniform."
What did he order?

De Night
Behint Chrissmiss

It vass de night behint Chrissmiss ven all tru de haus,
Nod a critter vass stirring, not eefen a maus.
Mine stockings ver hunk pie de chimpney uff rocks,
So dat Zanta coult zee I neeted new socks.
End de pubbies ver nestledt all snuck in der bets,
Vile wishins uff dog biscuits valtzed shrew der hets.
Mama in her kerchief und me in mine chaps,
Ver chust settlin dawn fer de colt vedder schnapps.
Ven awt on de lawn dare aroce sucha rumpus,
I sought it vass gankstas vot kum awt ta pump us!
So avay to de vinda I flew like a lark,
Bush oben de shudders und look awt in de dark.
Ven vot to mine vatering ice shouldt a beer,
Put a liddle olt slet und eight frisky reindeer.
Und a fat olt drifer mit rhett noce a tinkle,
I didn't know den it vass chust de Kris Krinkle.
More faster den eakles dare coursers day came,
So I call all my dogkies pie dare first names:
"Naw Fido! Naw Rofer! Naw Olaf! Naw Pixie!
"Here Vaggy, Here Venie, Here Vacky und Trixie!"
Und day race shrew de haus und awt de front door—
I'd sought I'd nefer see my dogkies no more.
Awt inta de front yart de pubbies day flewah,
Chased all de reindeer und de fat drifer toah!
Und ven day finely came pack I see at de clance,

Each iss cot in dare tease sum uff Zanta Glaus Bants!
De ice ha day twinkcult! Dare tailse vagging merry!
De rhett close in de mawth iss more den day ken carry!
So dot iss vhy Zanta left me no bresents dis year—
Chust vent pack to de Norse Bowl ta get batched in de
rear!
Und I hurt him essplain ass he drofe off in de night,
"Frum de front I look goot, put de pack iss a sight!"
—Frum an anunimus doner

Romeo und Chuliet

Scene Twoah—Gabulet's Carten

(Enta Romeo.)
Rom. He chests at scarse dat nefer felt a vound.—
  (Chuliet appearse abofe at a vinda.)
Putt, soft! Vhat light schru vonder vinda preaks?
It iss de east, und Chuliet iss de sun!—
Arice, fair sun, und kill de enwious moon,
Whoose already sick yet und bale viss crief,
Dat dowel her mate art far more fair den she;
Pee not her mate, since she iss enwious;
Her westal liffry is putt sick und creen,
Und nun putt follse do vear it; gast it off.—
It iss my lady; ach, it iss my luff!
Ach! Dat she vooda knowed she iss wunst!—
She speaks, yet she says nodding: vhat uff dat?
Her ice disgorses, I vill answer it.—
I'm too bolt, tiss not to me she speaks:
Twoah uff de fairest starse in all de heffen,
Haffing sum bissness, do make her ice
To twinkle in dare spears till day come back schru.
What iff her ice vere dare, day in her het?
De prightness uff her cheek vood shame doze starse,
Ass daylight duss a lamp; her ice in heffen
Vood shrew de airy reachin stream so pright
Dat berts vood sink, und sink it vass not night.—

See ha she leantce her cheek upon her hant,
Ach! Cheese und Grackers! Dat I vere a gluff upun
    dat hant,
Dat I might touch dat cheek wunst!

Chul. Ach! Dunna Wedda!

Rom. She brutzes:—
Ach, brutz again, pright anchel! Fer dowel art
As clorious to dis night, beink ova my het,
Ass iss a vinged messincher uff heffen
Unta de vite-upturnt ice dat wonder me so
Uff mortals dat fall pack to gase on him
Vhen he pestites de lacey-bacing clods
Und sailce upon de busum uff de air.

Chul. Ach naw! Romeo, Romeo! Vherefore art dowel,
    Romeo?
Deny die fodder und refuce die name;
Or, iff dowel vilt not, pee putt svorn my luff,
Und Al no lonker pee a Cabulet.

Rom. (Asite.) Shall I hear more, or shall I speak at
    dis?

Chul. Tiss putt die name dat iss my enemy;—
Dowel art dieself dough, not a Muntacue.
Vhat's Muntacue? It iss nor hant, nor foot,
Nor harm, nor face, nor any udder bart
Pelonking to a mann. Ach, pee sum udder name!
Vhat's in a name? Dat vhich ve call a roce,
Pie any udder name vood smell ass sveet;

So Romeo vood, vere he not Romeo calt,
Retain dat dear berfectshin vhich he ohce
Widdawt dat title:—Romeo, duff die name;
Und fer dat name, vhich iss no bart uff dee,
Take all myself.

Rom. Al take dee at die vort;
Call me putt luff und Al qvit my grexing
Und call myself Hinnerschnitz foreffermore.

Chul. Hinnerschnitz! I can't haff dat for a name! Dat roce vood not smell so sveet. Goot gruntbecky!

Rom. Get awt! Vhy you set yerself vhat's in a name.

Chul. I noah. I chest. Vhy, Hinnerschnitz vood be wonderful goot.

Rom. Vhy you liddle Nix Nootz! You hat me gone!

Chul. Hinnerschnitz, Hinnerschnitz! Come here wunst, Hinnerschnitz! Fer ve must smooch a hunnert times yet tonight!

Rom. Chuliet! Adchust die bunnit, for I cum hidder before de moon duss vane!

Sum Pomes for Reading Awt Lawd

Frum:
De Rafen

pi Etcur Allen Bo

Wunst upon a mittnight dreary, vile I pundert,
veek und veary,
Ova many a qvaint und gurious wolume
uff fergotten lore—
Vile I knotted, nearly nabbing,
suddenly dare came a tabbing,
Ass uff sum von chently rabbing,
rabbing at my champer door.
"Tiss sum wisitor," I muddered,
"tabbing at my champer door—
Only dis und nodding more."

Den, me sought, de air crew denser,
berfumed frum
n unseen censer
Swunk pie seraphim whoose footfalse
tinkled on de tufted floor.
"Vetch," I crite, "Die Got hass putt dee—
"Pie dese anchels he hass sent dee."
Respite—respite und nepence
frum die memries uff Lenore:
Qvaff, oh, qvaff dis kind nepence
und ferget dis lost Lenor!
Quoss de Rafen: "Nefermore!"

Frum:
Rupyat uff Omar Khayyam

A pook uff werses unternease de baw,
A chuck uff vine, a loaf uff bret, und dowel.

Pesite me sinking in de vilterness
Ach! Vilterness vere baradise naw!

Frum:
Ha Do I Luff Dee?

(Frum *Sunnits frum de Bortugeese*)
pi Elissabess Barrett Brawning

Ha do I luff dee? Let me cawnt de vase.
I luff dee to de depps und pretts und height
My soul ken reach, ven feeling awtta sight
Fer de ents uff Being und ideal Grace.
I luff dee to de leffel uff effry daze
Most qviet neat, by sun und cantlelight.
I luff dee freely, ass men strife fer Right
I luff dee burely, ass day turn frum Prace.
I luff dee viss de passhin pud to use
In my olt griefs, und viss my childthoot's face.
I luff dee viss a luff I seemed to loose,
Viss my lost saints—I luff dee viss de bress
Smals, tearce, uff all my life!—und, iff Got chews,
I shall putt luff dee bedder afta dess.

To Be Sunk
Awt Lawd

(For Your Sinking Enchoyment)

Piecycle Pilt Fer Twoah

Dare iss a flar vissin my heart,
Day-C! Day-C!
Blanted von day pie a clancing dart,
Planted pie Day-C Pell!
Vedder she luffs me or luffs me not,
Sometimese hit's hart to tell;
Yet I M lonking to share de lot,
Uff peautiful D-C Pell.
Day-C, Day-C,
Giff me yer answer do!
I'm half cray-C
All fer de luff uff youah!
It vohnt pee a stylish maritch,
I can't affort a caritch,
Put you'll look sveet,
Ubun de seat
Uff a piecycle pilt fer twoah!

Stant Up, Stant Up For Cheeses

Stant up, stant up for Cheeses,
ye soltiers uff de cross;
Lift high hiss royal banner, it muss not suffer loss
Frum wictry unto wictry, hiss army shall He leet,
Till effry foe iss wanquisht,
und Christ iss Lort indeet!

Stant up, stant up for Cheeses, de trumpet call opay,
Force to de mighty cunflict, in dis hiss clorious day.
"Ye dat are men naw surf him,
acainst unnumpert foes;
Let couritch rice viss dancher,
und strengt to strengt obbose.

She'll Be Cummin
Rawnd De Mawtin

She'll be cummin rawnd de mawtin ven she comess,
She'll be cummin rawnd de mawtin ven she comess,
She'll be cummin rawnd de mawtin, she'll be cummin
rawnd de mawtin,
She'll be cummin rawnd de mawtin ven she comess.

She'll be dryfin six vite horses ven she comess,
She'll be dryfin six vite horses ven she comess,
She'll be dryfin six vite horses, she'll be dryfin six
vite horses,
She'll be dryfin six vite horses ven she comess.

De Panned Plate On

K C vood valtz viss a strawburry blund,
Und de panned plate on,
He't glite cross de floor viss de girl he adort
Und de panned plate on,
Putt hiss prain vass so loatet it nearly essploted,
De boor curl vood shake viss alarms.
He't nefer leaf de curl viss de strawburry girlse,
Und de panned plate on.

Take Me Awt

(Sunk to de tune uff Take Me Awt To De Ballcame*)*

Take me awt to de Balony Fest
Take me awt to de fair
Feed me som picks's stummic und dippy X
Vhy eating dis stuff iss bedder den sex!
Chust rut rut rut for R Dutchie vase
Vhich to sum iss silly putt to us it's de pest!
It's von, twoah, schree laughs und yer awt
At de old Baloney Fest!

Dutchie

(De Dutchmen's Ansem)

(Sunk to de tune uff "Dixie," dat udder reachional fafrit)

I vish I vass in de lant uff Baloney,
Olt times dare R still not phoney,
Look avay, Look avay, Look avay, Dutchie lant.
In Dutchie lant vhere I vass porn in,
Hurley in von cloddy mornin,
Look avay! Look avay! Look avay! Dutchie lant.

Den I vish I vass in Dutchie lant,
Hooray! Hooray!
In Dutchie lant Al take my stant
To liff und die a Dutchman!
Avay, avay, avay back dawn schru in Dutch lant,
Avay, avay, avay back dawn schru in Dutch lant.

Dares shoo-fly pie and snitz und gnepp,
Makes you fat or a liddle fatter yet!
Look avay, Look avay, Look avay, Dutchie lant.
Den wootz it dawn und eat your scrapple,
To Dutchie lant I'm bond to traffel,
Look avay! Look avay! Look avay! Dutchie lant.

Receipts

Dese receipts really make. Try dem wunst!

Nana Emma's Shoo-Fly Pie

Make de crust same as for any udder pie, den pour in de fallowing mix-ups:

Mix up for de gook:
>   Von cup molassiss
>   Two cups brawn shooker
>   Von beaten eck
>   Two cups vodder
>   Von teasespoon bacon soda
>   (dissolfe in de vodder some)

>   Mix up for de crumps:
>   Schree cups flar
>   Von cup brawn shooker
>   Von-halve cup shortnin'

Sprinkle ova above. Bake at four hunnert decrees until dun.

Shooker Cakes

Incredients:
   4 cups sifted flar
   2 cups brawn shooker (pack tightly)
   ½ cup shortnin (part lart, part budder)
   1 teasespoon salt in flar

Miss vell viss a fork wunst.

Next part:
   2 X vell-beaten
   1 teasespoon wanilla in de milk
   ½ cup sick milk
   1 teasespoon brawn shooker in milk

Put in de milk by putting a liddle here and a liddle dare. Let stant ova night in a cool place.
   Worry de dough till it makes well.
   Miss vell effning before baking.

Santvich Spreat

Twelfe larch creen peffers
Twelfe larch rhett peffers
Twelfe creen tomatas
Twoah larch unyents

Grind, den scald, und let stant von quarter R. Drain, rescald, und let stant anudder quarter R. Drain wunst more yet.

At:
Schree taplespoon flar
2 small taplespoon salt
Schree cups gran shooker
½ class prepared musturd
1 qvart winegar diluted ½ viss vodder

Miss togedder und bake for 20 minutes.
Den at von bint mayonaisse.
Reheat und char.

Corn Cop Chelly

Get ten or twelfe bright rhett corn cops from somewhere (not frum an awthaus, naw!) und boil dem for sirty or forty-fife minutes. Strain! Den at fife cups shooker to schree cups chews.

Bring chews to a fast zimmer. At von bottle uff Certo; stir cunstintly for abawt four minutes. At shooker und boil rapidly until it is a chelly cunsistency. Pour in chars and seal.

Special note: Dare are some people dat put a short piece uff cop in each char, und pour da chelly ova it. It's so pretty!

Deffil's Foot Cake

Von eck
Von halb cup coco
Von und von halb cups flar
Von halb cup shortnin
Von halb cup sar milk
1 teasespoon wanilla
1 teasespoon sota
1 cup shooker
Von halb cup bolt vodder

Put in bowl in orter giffen. Do not miss until last item has been atted. Beat vell.

Chogalit Eyesing

1) 2 taplespoons coco
2) 1 cup bolt vodder
3) ¾ cup shooker
4) 1 taplespoon budder
5) ½ cup colt vodder
6) 2 taplespoons cornstarch
7) 1 teasespoon wanilla

Miss 1, 2, 3, 4; at to 5 and 6. Poil till sick. At 7 und spreat on de Deffil's Foot Cake. Surf togedder. (Or lick de eyesing und de batter outta de bowl before for a liddle extra fun.)

Boy Graut Pie
Plant Rhuparp Meringue

Schree cups boy grout
1 cup shooker
2 X
1 taplespoon tabioca
2 taplespoons budder

Miss shooker, x yokes, tabioca, and melted budder. Den miss vis rhuparp und put in unbaked pie shell und bake until pie plant is soft. Break eck vites und put on top und brawn.

Pick und Chighan Paddies

2 fistfulls uff flar
1 pinch uff B. P.
½ pinch uff salt
6 taplespoons shortnin
1 eck yoke slightly beaten
½ cup milk

Break da chighan's neck, or chop off its het viss an ax. After it stops running arawnd, defedder, and degut de bert. Take a pick already butchert, und use a favrit cut uff pick meat.

Sift dry incredients, at shortnin, und mix in soroughly viss a fork. At eck to milk. At to dry missture to make soft dough. Turn awt on flarred boart und toss lightly until de awtside looks smoose. Roll awt half dough inches sick. Cut inta quarters. Fit each inta muffin ban. Fill viss pick und chighan missture und folt de etches uff de pastry oafer de center. Pinch de etches togedder on de top. Repeat viss remaining. Bake in a hot offen 425 decrees von-sird R.

Abawt the Author

Gary Gates is a Dutchman from Lebanon County, Pennsylvania, where all the baloney comes from. People know where he is from when he opens his mouth.

Since you have bought this book for a price that comes to less than a penny a laugh, you have already gotten a bargain for your money. Therefore, we are not going to tell you any dull, pretentious, pompous things about the author, except to say that although he has a Master of Arts degree, he is still intelligent and a funny speaker. So instead of reading about him, you can get to know him by booking him. The police have booked him several times (for comedy shows), so why don't you? Gary can be bought cheap!

Gary is a performer, having appeared hundreds of times at festivals, fairs, colleges, libraries, corporation banquets, comedy clubs, writers groups, resorts, and on radio and TV. His Pennsylvania Dutch humor is riotous fun, sweet enough for family entertainment, yet salty enough to keep adults and children in stitches.

He loves performing and celebrating his unique heritage with his fellow Dutchmen, and sharing it with non-Dutchmen, whose response to his show has been overwhelmingly hysterical. Some people have declared him the new Professor Schnitzel, even the Mark Twain of Pennsylvania Dutch country. Even more people simply call him the best windbag they ever heard.